Crafts through the Year

Thomas and Petra Berger

Thomas and Petra Berger

Crafts through the Year

Floris Books

Translated by Polly Lawson

Photographs by Wim Steenkamp and Thomas
Berger. Illustrations by Ronald Heuninck
Transparencies by Petra Berger, Aeola Baan,
Sigrid Brandligt.

This collection first published in Dutch under the
title *Seizoenenknutselboek* by Christofoor Publishers
in 2000.
Parts of this book appeared in *The Easter Craft
Book* (1993), *The Harvest Craft Book* (1992) and
The Christmas Craft Book. (1990).

© 2000 by Christofoor Publishers, Zeist
This translation © Floris Books 2000
Second printing 2001

British Library CIP Data available

ISBN 0–86315–322-4

Printed in Belgium

Contents

Foreword

This book has been put together from parts of our earlier three books, *The Christmas Craft Book, The Easter Craft Book,* and *The Harvest Craft Book.* We now have a book with over 150 crafts through the year.

The season gradually follow each other in the eternal cycle of nature in the year. Many of the ideas here help to make visible indoors what is taking place outdoors.

After the long darkness of the winter months the buds on trees and bushes begin to swell. In her picture-book *The Story of the Root Children* Sibylle von Olfers tells in a most attractive way how the root-children wake from their sleep with Mother Earth and come up from the earth as flower-children.

Nature clothes herself in green leafs and a dazzling array of colourful blossoms which can be pressed and dried.

Depending on the warmth of the sun, the harvest begins in late summer. Harvest time offers a wealth of colourful material for craft activities.

As well as the development of the natural year we have the cycle of Christian festivals.

When nature begins to show life, it is the time of Easter, the festival of life overcoming death. It is a festival which, in one form or another, dates from long before the coming of Christianity. The Crucifixion and Resurrection are much too difficult for little children to grasp. For them it is enough to place before them symbols of new life in Nature: of eggs, chicks and lambs, and indeed also the Easter hare.

As spring merges into early summer, Christianity celebrates the festivals of Ascension and Whitsun. Both festivals are related to the sky and the air and the way living creatures open themselves to them. Symbols of this season are winged creatures (birds and butterflies) and the unfolding of flowers.

In summer, June 24 is the festival of St John, a time to live out in nature. It is a time for going out and gathering material (take a bag with you on every outing). Don't wait for autumn storms — many things are lying on the ground, without any need to plunder garden or park.

Ancient accounts and legends tell how the Archangel Michael was appointed by God the Father in heaven to undertake the battle with the dragon. He is not only the vanquisher of the dragon, but is also depicted as weighing of souls, as the one who stands at the gate of heaven weighing the harvest of a human life. His festival is on September 29.

Hallowe'en has its origin in the Celtic festival of Samhain, which celebrated the first day of winter on November 1. The spirits of the dead and other supernatural creatures — fairies, witches and goblins — were about on that night. Turnip and pumpkin lanterns are like the last afterthought of the summer's ripening strength.

Of all the festivals in the course of the year Christmas has a special place. This is the festival of the light that came to earth, the festival of the birth of the child Jesus. This is the festival which we celebrate afresh each year, which requires so much preparation, especially with children in the family. It is a challenge to make it peaceful amid all the rush.

The inner preparation for Christmas is best begun at the end of November or the beginning of December; that is, at the beginning of Advent, for Advent is the time of expectation and preparation.

Numbering of figures
To help locate the illustrations quickly the first part of their number refers to the page, the second the figure number on the page. Steps are shown as ①, ② and so on.

Finally a word of thanks to the many people who have stimulated us with their ideas. In presenting the many activities in this book, we hope very much that you will be encouraged to work with your children, and stimulated to produce your own variations and ideas.

Thomas and Petra Berger
Summer 2000

1 Spring

Mother Earth and the flower-children in coloured wool

❖ *Pipe-cleaners*
Unspun sheep's wool
"Magic wool" (clean, unspun, coloured, carded wool)

• Take four pipe-cleaners and make the head, arms and the upper body of Mother Earth (Figure 8-1) or of one of the flower-children.
① Make the arms by folding two of the pipe-cleaners in half.
② Twist them together.
③ To make the head and upper body, take a third pipe-cleaner and twist it round the arms.
④ Twist a fourth pipe-cleaner round the head and body to strengthen it.
• Tease out the unspun sheep's wool until it is very thin and twist it as tightly as possible round the arms. Keep on doing this until the arms have acquired the desired thickness. If necessary they can be made even thicker later on.

Figure 8-1. Mother Earth.

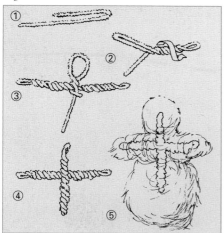

• Now begin winding wool round the head. Begin by taking as thin tufts as possible and ensure that the head becomes round. Make the head bigger than the length of the pipe-cleaner, as in ⑤.
• Unwashed sheep's wool has the advantage that the greasy wool binds together as it is wound round. If you don't have any, wind a thread over the wool from time to time to keep it firmly in place.
• Wind on to the lower body in the same way.
• Use coloured magic wool to dress the doll. Tease out this wool also as thinly as possible and wind it over the sheep's wool. Keep on doing this layer by layer until you can no longer see the foundation and the doll has acquired the desired colour (Figure 9-1).

Display the dolls in a safe place in the living-room. They are delicate and if you let children play with them too much the coloured magic wool will soon come away.

Figure 8-2. Flower children.

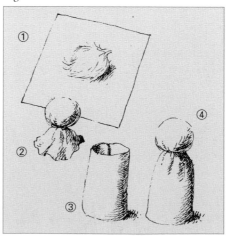

Flower-children made from felt

❖ *White or pink knitted cotton*
Unspun sheep's wool
Carded sheep's wool or "magic" wool
Pieces of felt in various colours

① For the head take a piece of knitted cotton 8 × 8 cm (3" × 3"). Make a little ball of the unspun wool about 2 cm (¾") diameter and place it in the centre of the piece of knitted cotton.
② Fold the knitted cotton round the ball of wool and tie it up round the neck.
③ For the body of the flower children you need a tube of felt. Take a rectangle of felt and sew two sides together. (The length and width of the body is different for each kind of flower-child.)
④ Gather in one of the open ends to make the neck. Stuff the loose material of the head into the gathered end of the tube, and sew neck and tube-body together.
• The doll will now stand as it is, but you can fill the tube with unspun wool and insert in the bottom a round piece of felt of the same colour as the tube, and sew it up.

This completes the basic form of all the flower-children. Now follow the details according to the kind of flower.

The crocus
• For the body take a piece of felt 6 × 6 cm (2¼" × 2¼").
① For the collar take a piece of light purple felt 10 × 3.5 cm (4" × 1½") and cut it out in the form shown in Figure 10-2. Gather in the upper edge and sew the collar round the neck.

Figure 9-1 >

② Do the same with the crocus' cap which can be of a darker purple. Gather in the felt a little at the place indicated so that the cap sits well on the head.

• Give the flower-child some hair in a colour matching the cap (for example with magic wool) before securing the cap on to the head with a few stitches. Then stitch the top edge of opposite pairs of petals together.

The snowdrop

• The snowdrop's body is 6 cm (2¼") high and 7 cm (2¾") wide.

① Cut out the light green collar (Figure 10-3), pucker it and sew it on to the body.

② The snowdrop's cap consists of three separate white petals. Sew the tops of the petals on to a little stalk of light green felt ③.

• First give the flower-child's head some hair of white wool before sewing on the cap with a few stitches.

The tulip

• The tulip's body is 5.5 cm (2½") high and 10 cm (4") wide.

① Cut out the red collar (Figure 10-4), pucker it and sew it on to the body.

② The tulip-child has a cap made of six separate red petals. Sew the first two petals to the side of the head.

③ Gather in the remaining four petals below before sewing them on to the head overlapping each other. Give the tulip pink hair.

The daffodil

• The body of the daffodil is about 5 cm (2") high and 10 cm (4") wide.

① Cut out the yellow collar (Figure 10-4), pucker it and sew it on to the body.

② The daffodil's cap has two parts. First sew the puckered yellow petal wreath on to the head.

③ Cut out a round piece from the dark yellow felt to make the heart of the flower. Cut into the disc in two places and sew it up so that it bulges out. Sew the heart on to the crown of the head.

Figure 10-2. Crocus.

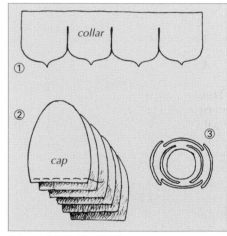

Figure 10-4. Tulip.

Figure 10-1.

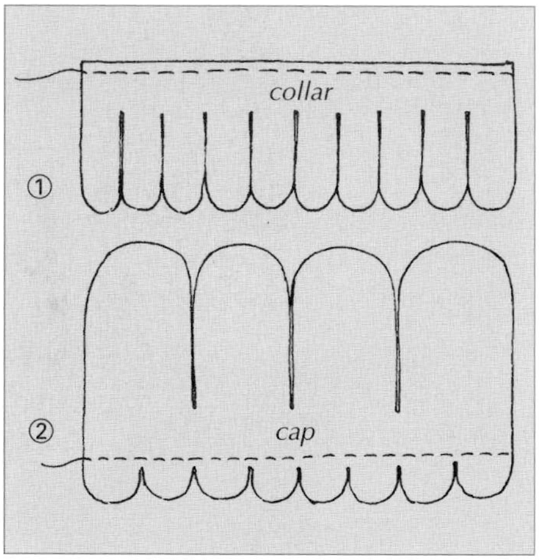

Figure 10-3. Snowdrop. ∨

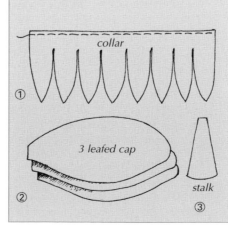

Figure 10-5. Daffodil. ∨

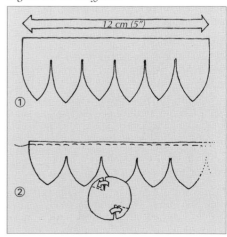

*Simple variation for
the flower-children*
You can buy little dolls of natural
wood which have just a head and
body. They come in various sizes. You
can dress these wooden dolls quite
simply by sticking bits of felt on to
them.

Transparency made of
modelling wax

❖ *A pane of glass or perspex
   Blocks of modelling wax in various
      colours
   Strips of decorating wax in various
      colours
   A hot-water bottle*

This transparency is made on glass or
perspex. Perspex has the advantage
that it is a light-weight substance and
that you can hang up the transparency
immediately, simply drilling small
holes in the corners. With glass you
will generally have to give it a lead
frame with a hook so that it can be
hung up.

• You can of course create a transparency freely, but if you have not had
much practice it is better to first make
a sketch on paper.

• Don't let the drawing become too
intricate. If the sketch is to full size
you can stick it to the back of the
pane.

   Modelling wax is a coloured transparent wax which softens when knead-
ed gently; the softened wax is then
easy to shape and can be pressed
straight on to the pane. Stockmar decorating wax comes in thin strips and
can be applied without further ado.

   Making a transparency with modelling wax requires time and patience.
One advantage is that you have time
to observe what shapes are emerging,
and can vary the picture accordingly,
despite the sketch.

• Take small pieces of wax because
they are quicker to soften and you can
cover large areas more easily.

• As soon as you put the wax on to
the glass or perspex it immediately
cools down and becomes hard,
making it difficult to spread into a
thin transparent layer. You may find
it helpful to keep the glass or perspex

Figure 11-1. Transparency made with modelling wax.

11

warm by laying it on a hot-water bottle.

• Apply the wax thinly as you can always apply a second layer or press the wax together to obtain a darker colour. From time to time hold up the pane to the window to see how it will look where it will eventually be hung.

A picture made of magic wool

❖ *A piece of cambric or other roughly woven fabric*
Magic wool

Magic wool is fine carded sheep's wool which is obtainable in packets with many different colours. The wool will stick by itself on to a rough backing such as cambric or ribbed velvet.

• First select a suitable colour of cambric as backing, depending on the colour of the wool which you are going to use. Cambric comes in many colours.

• Hem round the edges of the cambric and lay the cloth on to a table, on a

Figure 12-1. Picture with magic wool.

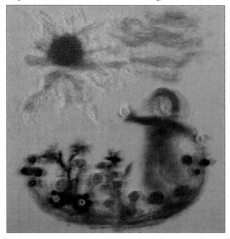

board or soft-board, or secure it straight on to the wall.

• Tease out the magic wool thinly, shape the wool and press it on to the backing. The thicker the magic wool the more intense the colours will be (Figure 12-1).

• You can always refashion part of the picture as it is easy to remove the wool from the backing. This is what makes magic wool so easy to use — you can always change the picture, for instance, with the seasons.

• If you are not intending to change the picture or want it as a gift, secure the tufts of magic wool with a few thread stitches.

Palm Sunday branches

❖ *Some branches*
Crêpe-paper
Green sprigs of box (optional)
Button-thread or thin wire or florist's wire
Cane
A cockerel made of dough and/or paper
Dried fruits: raisins, dried apples, dried apricots

The procession with Palm Sunday branches is a very ancient custom in memory of Christ's entry into Jerusalem, when the people took branches from the trees and laid them on his pathway.

In the past in Europe each region had its own model of Palm Sunday branch. Here we have two basic forms: the branch with a round hoop, and the branch in the form of a cross.

The symbol of the cross, reminding of the Crucifixion, can be difficult for little children to understand. For them a branch with a hoop is a sign of approaching spring, the circle being a symbol of the sun and the light.

A Palm Sunday branch with a round hoop

In the Palm Sunday branch shown in Figure 13-1 the stick is wrapped in light green crêpe-paper and decorated with dark green crêpe-paper.

• Make sure that the Palm Sunday branch is not too heavy. For little children don't make the stick longer than the child's stretched arm's length.

• Make the hoop with cane. Form a loop about 30–40 cm (12"–15") in diameter and then tie them firmly.

• Let the children help with making and decorating the Palm Sunday sticks.

• Decorate the hoop with streamers of crêpe-paper and dried fruits.

• Finally bind the hoop to the stick with strong twine or thin wire, and put the cockerel in its place on top.

The Palm Sunday branch in the form of a cross

• Find two suitable branches with the horizontal branch half the length of the vertical. Notch both branches lightly where they are to cross and tie them together with thin wire or strong twine.

• Put it in a stable vase or in a box filled with sand so that it will stand upright when decorating it.

• The Palm Sunday branch in Figure 13-2 is partially decorated with green from a box bush. (Many hedges are box, as it remains green throughout the year.) Take care when binding on the box twigs to keep them facing in the same direction because the underside and the topside of the leaves are different in colour.

• Then stick coloured crêpe-paper on

to the horizontal branch so that each end gets a brush of box twigs.

• Now hang streamers of crêpe-paper on to the horizontal branch. As shown in Figure 13-2 the strips of crêpe-paper (about 2 cm (¾") wide) have been nicked on each side to allow more lively movement.

• Finally you can decorate the branch with an orange into which box twigs have been inserted. Cut the top of the branch to a point so that the Palm Sunday cockerel can be set there.

For baking a dough cockerel see page 17.

A paper Palm Sunday cockerel

❖ *Thin white card*
Coloured pencils or crayons
Adhesive

Children will soon eat the dough cockerel on top of the Palm Sunday branch making it look rather bare. So get them to first make a paper cockerel (Figures 13-4 and 13-5).

• From the card cut out two cockerels with good fat bellies, and cut a thin strip about 2 cm (¾") wide.

• Let the children to colour the two cockerels so that one is the mirror-image of the other as they will then be stuck together.

• Make a little tube from the strip of card so that it fits over the point of the branch.

① Stick the top edges of the cockerels together and insert it between the bottom edges, and glue it in ②. As soon as the dough cockerel has disappeared the paper cockerel can take its place on top of the branch.

Figure 13-3. Baked cockerel.

Figure 13-1. Branch with round hoop.

Figure 13-2. Branch in form of cross.

Figures 13-4 ∧   13-5 ∨   Paper cockerel.

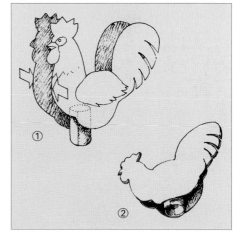

13

2 A Festive Table

An Easter tree

❖ *Branches*
  Green sprigs of box
  Thin wire or strong thread
  12 decorated blown-out eggs

• Find suitable branches for this Easter tree. Figure 14-2 shows possible measurements.
• Notch the places where the branches cross and tie them securely with strong thread or wire.
• Decorate the tree with sprigs of box. It helps to put the tree in a stable vase or into a box with sand.
• Now carefully hang the blown-out eggs on to the tree: on the highest branch hang one egg on each side, on the middle branch two eggs and on the lowest branch three eggs on each side. Leave the tree to stand in the vase or pot or fix it in a wooden base to keep it upright. Alternatively, put the tree in a box with early spring flowers.

Easter branches with eggs

❖ *One or more green leafy branches*
  Blown-out decorated eggs
  Thread or very fine wire

You can make a very festive Easter decoration for a room by hanging coloured blown-out eggs on a branch or two.
• Four weeks before Easter select suitable branches with buds and put them in water in a vase in a warm room. By Easter the buds will have opened and fresh green leaves will have come out.
• At Easter decorate the branches with some beautifully decorated blown-out eggs.

A box or eggshell with cress

❖ *A box filled with earth*
  An eggshell
  A bag of cress-seed
  A plastic sheet

Sowing cress in a box lets children see plants sprouting in spring. Already after one to two days cress will sprout and after about a week it is ready for eating.
• Moisten the earth in the box well.
• Spread the cress-seed evenly over the soil (and if your house is very dry cover the box with a thin plastic sheet which is removed when the seeds sprout).
• In the warm humid atmosphere of the box the seeds should soon sprout. Take away the plastic once the seeds have sprouted.
• Now the children can watch how the cress grows daily until a tiny leaf appears on the end of each stalk. Make sure that the soil remains damp.

As a decoration for the Easter table you can also sow the cress in an eggshell.

Figure 14-1. An Easter tree.

Figure 14-2. Measurements for Easter tree.

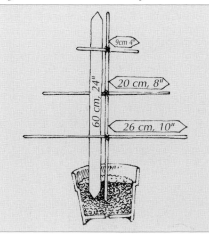

Figure 15-1 >

- Remove the top of a boiled egg carefully. The rest of the shell makes a little container which can be filled with earth.
- To get a smooth round edge to the shell, first score gently round the eggshell with a fine metal-saw and then break the shell carefully.

Home-made egg-cups

❖ *Empty toilet paper rolls*
Coloured paper
Glue

- Take an empty toilet roll and cut out a number of rings 1.5–2 cm (¾") wide.
- Stick some coloured tissue or other paper on to the rings. Alternatively stick white paper on to the rings and let the children colour them. In this way each child can make their own egg-cup for Easter.

Folding an egg-cup

❖ *Square sheets of paper about 12 × 12 cm (5" × 5")*
Glue

- Fold a sheet in half in both directions. Open out again, turn it over, and repeat diagonally (Figure 16-3).
① Bring the four corners together by folding B and C simultaneously on to point D. Point A will follow on top.
② Fold point A to the line EF.
③ Then fold along EF.
- Turn over and repeat with point D.
④ Fold the top point F across to E and the lower point E to point F. Turn the whole thing round 180° so that point G comes to the bottom.
- Fold points F and E to the centre line. Repeat this for the back.
⑤ Fold point H to the bottom and tuck the point in as shown. Do the same for the back. Now the egg-cup is almost finished.
⑥ Open out the top carefully so

Figure 16-1. Eggshell with cress.

Figure 16-2. Home-made egg-cups.

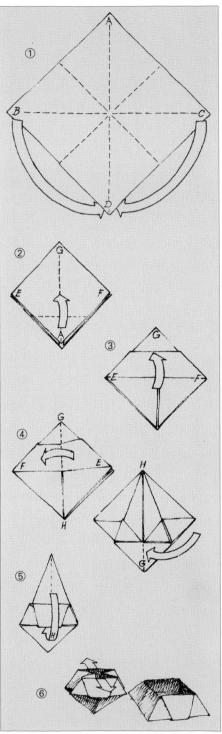

Figure 16-3. Folding an egg-cup.

16

that the point at the bottom gradually disappears and becomes the base of the egg-cup.

Variation

Of course you can make the folded egg-cup from coloured origami paper or from a sheet of white paper which the children have painted or coloured beforehand. In this case start with the coloured side of the sheet face up, and at the first stage, fold the coloured side into itself. The small square is white now, but the coloured side will end up on the outside.

3 Dough Figures

A recipe for dough

❖ *about 500 g (1 lb) white or wholemeal flour or a mixture of both*
½ tablespoon of yeast dissolved in 300 ml (10 fl oz) lukewarm milk (not more than 30°C, 85°F)
50 g (1¾ oz) hard butter
½ tablespoon salt
3 tablespoons sugar
½ tablespoon aniseed

The recipe will make eight hares, or nests, or little men, and so on.
• Keep about 100 g (4 oz) of flour back and put the rest into a bowl. Make a hole in the middle and pour the yeast mixture into it. Stir from the middle outwards taking in some of the flour to make a sloppy paste.
• Cut the butter up into very thin slices and lay these on to this yeast-mixture. Sprinkle the salt, sugar and aniseed over the butter. Put the bowl into a plastic bag and allow the mixture to rise to twice its volume at room temperature; this can take twenty minutes or more.
• Take half of the flour which you have kept back. Sprinkle it over the mixture and at the same time work it into the mixture with the salt, sugar, aniseed and the butter which in the meantime has become soft.
• Empty this loose dough on to a board which has been sprinkled with flour and knead it (not too long) until it no longer sticks to your hand and feels firm but still soft and elastic. Knead the dough with the heel of your hand giving it a quarter turn now and again.
• Put the dough back into the bowl, place in a fridge or cool place, and allow it to rise to about twice its volume. This will take three to four

hours. Cold dough can be shaped better.
• The forming of the risen dough is described under each separate figure.
• To finish off pre-heat the oven. Before baking brush the figures with loosely beaten egg or with egg-yolk loosely whisked with some milk.

Bake about 20 minutes at 225°C (435°F, gas mark 7), middle rack.

A cockerel for the Palm Sunday branch

• Make a dough as in the recipe.
• Divide the risen dough into eight portions and roll out each portion to a strip about 18 cm (7") long.
• Bend the strips round as you lay them on a baking tray, making the tail-piece a bit shorter than the head-piece.

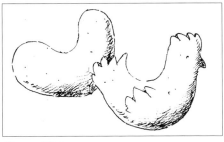

Figure 17-1.

• Make sure that there is enough space between each portion to allow for rising and above all make the figures *thin;* for when they rise they will become thicker.
• With a sharp pair of scissors cut twice into the dough to make the beak, pull out this piece and smooth

off the cut.
- Cut into both ends to make the comb and the tail and indicate the wings with single cuts.
- Finally take a sharp knife and make a hole for the eye and put a raisin or currant into the hole.
- You can decorate the dough-cockerel with nuts or such like.

Little bread men

- Make a dough as in the recipe.
- Divide the risen dough into eight portions.
① Make each portion into a pear-shape.
② With a sharp knife cut slits to form arms and legs. Notch the eye-sockets and insert two raisins to make the eyes.
③ Take a hard-boiled egg, place it on the man's stomach and fold his arms over it.
- Use only those eggs which have been coloured in a plant-dye bath, otherwise the dye may come away on to the bread.

Figure 18-1. Little bread men.

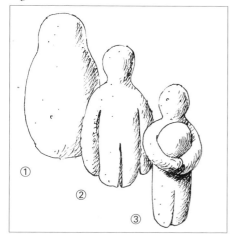

A fruit-cake Easter hare or lamb

For this you will need a special two-part baking form (Figure 18-2) in the shape of a hare or lamb (to hold ½ litre, 1 pint).

❖ 200 g (7 oz) wholemeal
½ tablespoon yeast dissolved in
100 ml (3½ fl oz) milk
about 50–75 g (2 oz) hard butter
½ teaspoon salt
25 g (1 oz) cane sugar or syrup, dis-solved in
1 yolk of an egg in half an eggshell of water
the grated peel of half a lemon
about 60 g (2 oz) sliced dates without stones

- Put the meal into a bowl and make a hollow in the middle. Pour the yeast mixture into the hollow and stir it with some of the meal into a runny paste. Lay the butter in thin slices on top and sprinkle with the salt.
- Put the bowl into a plastic bag and allow it to stand at room temperature until bubbles appear in the mixture (20 minutes or longer).
- Pour the egg-sugar syrup over the butter which has become soft and add the grated lemon peel. Stir and beat the whole from the middle outwards to a smooth moist dough for 5 min-utes.
- Mix in the dates, put the bowl back into the plastic bag and allow the dough to rise to twice its volume. At room temperature this will take at least two hours and it does not matter if it takes longer.
- Take the baking form apart and grease the two halves by brushing with softened butter. Sprinkle flour over it and knock out the surplus flour.
- Fill the forms making sure that the ears and head are well filled before continuing and close them together.

Put the form on a baking-tray into a pre-heated oven.
    Bake for about 30 minutes at 190°C (375°F, gas mark 5) bottom rack.
- After removing from the oven leave the form closed for five minutes, then free the edges with a knife before care-fully opening. Put the hare or lamb on to a grid to cool off.
- Shortly before serving cut the base level so that the animal will stand and sprinkle with icing-sugar.

Figure 18-2. Baking forms for a hare.

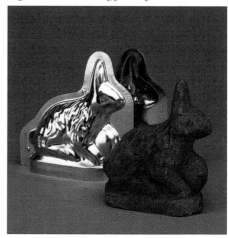

Figure 18-3. Knotted cloth hare.

4 Working with Wool and Textiles

The symbol of the Easter hare is ancient. In Germanic mythology the hare brings the new seeds of life (eggs) to the earth. The hare is an animal which has no burrow and does not live in herds. It sleeps under the open sky and leaves its young spread out in well sheltered places. In fairy tales we often find the picture of the hare rescuing other animals by sacrificing itself.

Figure 19-1. Knotted cloth hare.

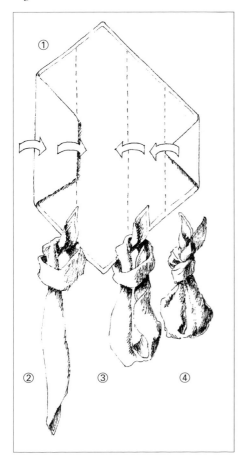

A knotted cloth hare

❖ *A soft square piece of cloth*

① Fold the cloth over diagonally.
② Tie a loose knot in one end.
③ Then bring the other end through the loop of the knot to make two ears.
④ Pull the knot a bit tighter, pull the whole thing out a bit and there you have the hare (Figure 18-3).

Woollen chickens

❖ *Stiff cardboard*
  A pair of compasses
  A large darning-needle
  Yellow or white knitting wool or lace thread
  Scraps of orange felt
  Button thread

Each little chick is made of two pom-poms of wool, one large and one small.
● Take the compasses and draw following circles on the cardboard: two small ones with a radius of 18 mm (0.7") with a tiny circle inside of about 5 mm (0.2") radius, and two with a radius of 26 mm (1"), and a little circle with a radius of 17 mm (0.3") inside.
① Cut out the circles so that you get rings with a hole in the middle. Cut into the rings in one place.
② Take a strong thread (or wool, if it is strong enough) and make it into a double loop. Lay the loop on one of the cardboard rings and lay the second ring of the same size on top of it, ensuring the cuts in the rings don't lie on top of each other. Let the ends of the loop hang down outside the rings.

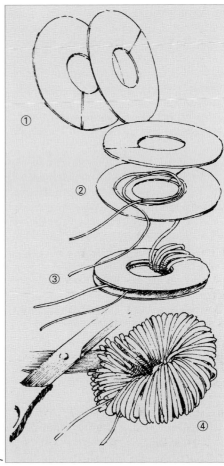

Figure 19-2. Pattern for woollen chicken.

Figure 19-3. Woollen chickens.

③ Wind the wool loosely (by hand or with a darning needle) round the rings until the hole in the centre is filled up.

④ Push a scissor blade between the two rings and cut the wool round the outside. Draw the loop which was laid between the rings tight and tie it up firmly. Do not cut the ends of the loop yet.

• As the rings were cut you can now carefully remove them so that they can be used again. Trim the pompom.

• Make the other pompom in the same way and tie the two together with the loose loop-threads.

• Finally cut out one or two orange felt triangles and tie them to the smaller pompom for the beak.

• Of course you can make a whole brood of chicks.

Woollen rabbits

❖ *Stiff cardboard*
A pair of compasses
Brown knitting wool
Scraps of brown felt
A large darning-needle

Figure 20-1. Woollen rabbit.

The rabbits are made in the same way as the chicks described above.

• The smaller ring has a radius of 21 mm (0.85") and a hole of 7 mm (¼") radius; the larger ring has a radius of 35 mm (1.4") and a hole of 13 mm (½") radius.

• Tie the pompoms together, cut out two ears from some felt and sew them on to the head. For the eyes take two black beads and sew them loosely to the head.

• With these rather larger rings you can also use unspun brown wool. For this card the wool in thin long wisps. These rabbits made of unspun sheep's wool have to be trimmed rather more.

A knitted chicken

❖ *Yellow wool*
Knitting needles 2–2½ mm (American size 1)
Unspun sheep's wool
Red wool for the comb

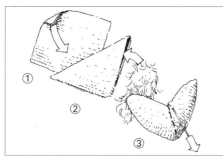

Figure 20-2.

① Cast on 16 stitches and knit a Knit plain each way so that there are ribs. Cast off.

② Fold the piece over diagonally and sew up one of the sides. Sew the other side only half up. Fill the body with unspun wool and finish sewing up the side.

③ Shape the chicken by running a thread from the point of the underside round the hen's middle. Draw in the thread lightly, and secure: this will pull the head and tail up.

• Use a yarn of red wool with the button-hole stitch to make the comb and the gills.

• To make the eyes take a length of darker wool or a bead.

Knitted Easter hare egg-cosy

❖ *Brown knitting wool*
Knitting-needles 3–3½ mm (American size 3)
Unspun sheep's wool
Brown and pink felt
Embroidery thread
Two beads for the eyes

• Cast on 20 to 28 stitches depending on the thickness of the wool. The length should go round an egg-cup comfortably. With very thin wool use double yarn. Knit a piece of about 18 ribs (36 plain rows). Do not cast off, but string the stitches on to the knitting yarn, pull tight and break off.

Figure 20-3. Knitted chicken.

- Sew up the long side to make a tube. Stuff it one third full with some unspun wool to make the head. Tie up the neck with a length of wool and shape the head so that the nose runs to a point.
- For the ears use two pieces of felt. Make the pink felt piece a little smaller and sew it on to the brown felt. Fold the felt ears together at the bottom, and sew them on to the head.
- Embroider the eyes or use two beads. Finally embroider the nose and give the hare a few side-whiskers.

Felt egg-cosy

❖ *Pieces of felt*
Embroidery-thread

The Figure below shows an egg-cosy with flowers. The flowers are cut out from felt and sewn on to the background. Of course this kind of egg-cosy can be made in all sorts of different ways, also by working just with embroidery thread on the felt.
- Cut out two pieces according to the

pattern at the end of the book in Figure 115-2.
- Decorate one or both sides in your own way and sew the two pieces together.

Felt hen egg-cosy

❖ *Yellow felt in two shades*
Red felt for the comb and beak
Unspun sheep's wool
Beads for the eyes
Embroidery thread

- Cut out the body twice, the wings twice, the beak twice, and the comb once according to the pattern at the end of the book in Figure 115-1.
- Sew the wings on to the body. Then sew the two halves of the hen's body together with the buttonhole-stitch, stitching the comb between the two parts. Finish off the bottom also with the buttonhole-stitch.
- Sew the two red beaks into place and fill the head with some unspun wool.
- Finally sew the beads into place as eyes.

An Easter hare as a finger-puppet

❖ *Thin knitting wool*
Knitting-needle 2 mm (American size 0)
Unspun sheep's wool
Two beads for the eyes
Embroidery thread
A little egg

- Cast on 20 stitches and knit 20 rows 1 row plain 1 row purl for the body. Then knit 10 rows 1 row purl and 1 row plain (reversing the pattern) to make the head.
- Do not cast off, but run them on to the knitting yarn. Pull the yarn tight and break off.
- Sew up the long edge, so that the head is ribbed on the outside. Fill the head with unspun wool turning the front edge outwards a little to make a proper nose. Tie up the neck with a length of wool.
- For the ears cast on 8 stitches and knit 10 rows 1 row plain 1 row purl. On the eleventh row decrease by knitting 4 times 2 stitches together. Knit the twelfth row purl. Knit the thirteenth row twice two stitches together. Cast off.

Figure 21-1. Knitted egg-cosy.

Figure 21-2. Felt egg-cosy.

Figure 21-3. Felt-hen egg-cosy.

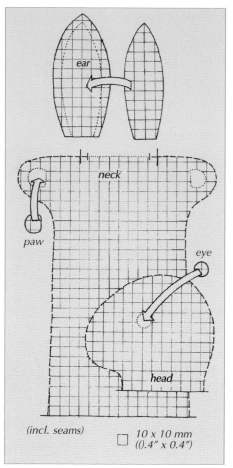

Figure 22-1. Pattern for glove puppet.

(incl. seams)

□ 10 x 10 mm
(0.4" x 0.4")

ear

neck

paw

eye

head

• Sew up the sides and sew the ears on to the head in such a way that the seam is at the back.
• For the rucksack cast on 16 stitches and knit 8 rows plain. Run the stitches on to the knitting yarn, pull the yarn tight and break off.
• Sew the rucksack on to the back, securing the yarn crosswise with a few stitches to make the rucksack-straps.
• Embroider a nose, give the hare some side-whiskers and sew the beads in place for eyes (Figure 22-2).
• Finally place a small egg in the rucksack.

An Easter hare as a glove puppet

❖ Pieces of fabric, preferably knitted cotton for the body
Pieces of pink felt for the inside of the ears and paws
Brown felt for the eyes
Unspun sheep's wool
Embroidery-thread

• Select a suitable piece of the material and cut out head, body and the ears each twice (Figure 22-1).

• First sew the pink front on to the ears. Sew the sides together inside out and turn them. The bottom is thus still open.
• Sew the eyes on to the separate halves of the head. Sew the halves inside out on to each other leaving the neck open. Turn the right side out.
• Then embroider the pink inside of the paws on to the two pieces of the body. Sew together the two halves of the body inside-out leaving the bottom and the neck open. Turn the body right side out, and hem the bottom.
• Now all the separate pieces can be sewn together. First sew the head into the neck of the body and then the ears on to the head.
• Finish off the Easter hare by filling the head with some unspun wool and make a hole in the wool with your finger so that later a finger will fit in when the hare is played with. Finally give the animal an embroidered nose and side-whiskers.

Figure 22-2. Finger puppets.

Figure 22-3. Glove puppet.

Figure 22-4. Egg decorated by children.

5 Decorating Easter Eggs

Decorating eggs is a custom which goes back to before the beginnings of recorded history. The egg was seen as the symbol for germinating power and new life.

There are many ways of decorating Easter eggs. The method depends on what you want to do with the eggs. Are they going to be eaten or just used for decoration?

If they are to be eaten we can decorate boiled egg before they come on to the Easter breakfast table or are hidden in the garden. The decoration is short-lived and for once only.

For decoration a blown-out egg can be hung on an Easter tree or blossoming branch, for the whole time from Easter to Ascension. You can even keep blown-out eggs carefully for another year.

For some of the methods, for example with batik, you will have to immerse the egg in a liquid. This is not really suitable for blown-out eggs, and is better used for eggs which have been very hard boiled (half an hour or more), so that they don't spoil so quickly.

Before beginning to decorate

The quality of the eggshell can differ greatly; so check whether it is too thin (it can crack or break while it is being boiled or blown out) and check whether the surface is nice and smooth.

White eggs are the best for decorating but they are often hard to obtain.
• Eggshells are always a bit greasy. To enable the paint or colouring to stick properly the grease should first be removed from the egg with some vinegar or washing-up liquid.
• Make a hole in the top and bottom of the egg with a pin or an egg-pricker.
• These holes are still too small to let you blow the egg out, so take two large round nails, one about 2 mm ($^1/_{12}$") thick and the other about 4 mm ($^1/_5$") thick. Sharpen the points of the nails so that they can serve as a kind of drill.
• Make one of the holes in the egg just a little larger (the hole you blow through) and use the thin nail at the other end to make the hole bigger (Figure 23-1).
• Blow the egg out over a jar (use it for scrambled eggs or omelettes), then rinse out the inside of the eggshell a little by letting some water flow in through the hole and blowing it out again, or by taking some water into your mouth and blowing it through the egg. This is to ensure that no residue is left in the shell.
• Make sure that no water remains in the shell to avoid problems while you are painting the egg.
• Figure 23-2 shows a very simple gadget, Blas-fix, which makes the blowing-out of eggs much easier, by only requiring one hole and no blowing.

Figure 23-1. Making holes

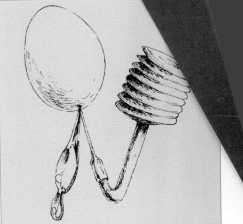

Figure 23-2. A Blas-fix.

Batik variation
When eggs have to be left for some time submerged in a bath of hot dye, make the larger hole bigger with the thicker nail. This is done by twisting the nail slowly round applying light pressure: the sharp edges cut into the egg without breaking it. The dye can now enter the eggshell and it stays submerged.

Hanging up the eggs

① After the egg is decorated tie the end of a length of thread firmly around the middle of half a match-stick (or wire) and poke the match with the thread through the hole in the egg. Now pull the thread carefully and the match will come to rest across the hole and will not come out any more.

② If the egg has two slightly larger holes you can run a thin ribbon right through the egg and tie a bow in it at the bottom of the egg.

● Now the egg can be hung up.

< *Figure 24-1.*

Figure 25-1. Methods of hanging eggs.

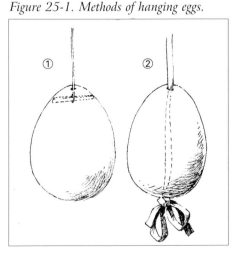

Eggs to be decorated by children

❖ *Coloured pencils or*
  Wax crayons

Decorating eggs with coloured pencils or wax crayons is very simple (Figure 22-4). For children thick crayons or block-crayons are best. Even the smallest children can take part.

Note that blown-out eggs are very fragile and can easily be squashed by young children. Hard boiled eggs are more suitable.

Colouring eggs with plant dyes

❖ *Tea, coffee, camomile, onion skin, juice from spinach, beetroot and so on.*

Everyday plant-products used in the kitchen are suitable for dying eggs, such as tea-leaves, coffee, camomile and onion skin, or vegetables like spinach and beetroot. Exotic plants and insect-dyes such as tumeric from India sandalwood from Africa, or cochineal from the West Indies will also produce very beautiful colours. Some of these products are sold as egg-dyes. In general they need only a short time on the boil (see also "Materials" on page 116).

● Put the material to make the dye into a pot of cold water and bring to a boil. Then carefully immerse the thoroughly cleaned egg into the boiling water. Of course white eggs will take on better colours than brown eggs.

● With some materials, like coffee and tea, first bring the water to boiling before adding the material. Leave to boil for a short time before immersing the eggs.

● You will have to experiment a bit first especially with the length of time for boiling.

● Plant dyes cannot be used indefinitely. After five or six eggs have been boiled in them the colour begins to fade. Use a small saucepan and make sure that the eggs are fully immersed, or turn them over regularly.

You can get a whole range of colours. They can be made more intense by a dash of vinegar.

— *light yellow:* camomile flowers, marigold petals
— *light brown:* onion skin (five to ten minutes)
— *dark brown:* strong black tea or coffee
— *red:* beetroot juice is very good, pokeberries
— *green:* boiled liquid of spinach or nettles
— *violet:* huckleberries, grapes

● Once the eggs have dried off thoroughly after their colour-bath they can be rubbed with a cloth dipped in salad oil. This will give them a soft sheen and the colour will not rub off so easily.

The eggs on the Easter tree in Figure 14-1 were coloured with plant dyes.

Painting eggs with water-colours

❖ *Paints (water-colours, poster colours or plant dyes)*
  Paint brushes
  Wooden barbecue sticks or thin knitting needles
  A piece of wire
  A little modelling wax

One of the difficulties of painting an egg with water-colours (artists or poster) is how to hold it so that you

25

Figure 26-1. Colours scratched away.

Figure 26-2. Stamped eggs.

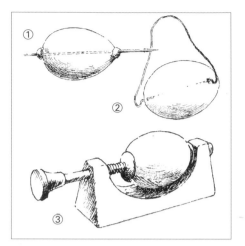

Figure 26-3.

don't put your fingers on the wet painted part, and yet being able to keep turning the egg round as you paint. There are several ways of overcoming this difficulty.

① One simple way is to push a long wooden barbecue stick (or thin knitting needle) through both holes and secure it with a bit of modelling wax.

② Another way is to bend a bit of wire so that it acts as a pair of tongs with each end of the wire inserted in the holes of the egg.

③ Finally there are egg-holders on the market which hold the egg. The holder comes with six different watercolours made of natural substances, which are safe for young children.

• You can simply paint the egg or first put it into a colour-bath to provide a background colour. Use the paint fairly thickly. If it is too thin, it will run on the round, non-porous surface of the egg.

• Once the eggs are thoroughly dry apply a coat of varnish so that the colours will not subsequently run.

• Sew up the long side to make a tube. Stuff it one third full with some unspun wool to make the head. Tie up the neck with a length of wool and shape the head so that the nose runs to a point.
• For the ears use two pieces of felt. Make the pink felt piece a little smaller and sew it on to the brown felt. Fold the felt ears together at the bottom, and sew them on to the head.
• Embroider the eyes or use two beads. Finally embroider the nose and give the hare a few side-whiskers.

Felt egg-cosy

❖ *Pieces of felt*
 Embroidery-thread

The Figure below shows an egg-cosy with flowers. The flowers are cut out from felt and sewn on to the background. Of course this kind of egg-cosy can be made in all sorts of different ways, also by working just with embroidery thread on the felt.
• Cut out two pieces according to the pattern at the end of the book in Figure 115-2.
• Decorate one or both sides in your own way and sew the two pieces together.

Felt hen egg-cosy

❖ *Yellow felt in two shades*
 Red felt for the comb and beak
 Unspun sheep's wool
 Beads for the eyes
 Embroidery thread

• Cut out the body twice, the wings twice, the beak twice, and the comb once according to the pattern at the end of the book in Figure 115-1.
• Sew the wings on to the body. Then sew the two halves of the hen's body together with the buttonhole-stitch, stitching the comb between the two parts. Finish off the bottom also with the buttonhole-stitch.
• Sew the two red beaks into place and fill the head with some unspun wool.
• Finally sew the beads into place as eyes.

An Easter hare as a finger-puppet

❖ *Thin knitting wool*
 Knitting-needle 2 mm (American size 0)
 Unspun sheep's wool
 Two beads for the eyes
 Embroidery thread
 A little egg

• Cast on 20 stitches and knit 20 rows 1 row plain 1 row purl for the body. Then knit 10 rows 1 row purl and 1 row plain (reversing the pattern) to make the head.
• Do not cast off, but run them on to the knitting yarn. Pull the yarn tight and break off.
• Sew up the long edge, so that the head is ribbed on the outside. Fill the head with unspun wool turning the front edge outwards a little to make a proper nose. Tie up the neck with a length of wool.
• For the ears cast on 8 stitches and knit 10 rows 1 row plain 1 row purl. On the eleventh row decrease by knitting 4 times 2 stitches together. Knit the twelfth row purl. Knit the thirteenth row twice two stitches together. Cast off.

Figure 21-1. Knitted egg-cosy.

Figure 21-2. Felt egg-cosy.

Figure 21-3. Felt-hen egg-cosy.

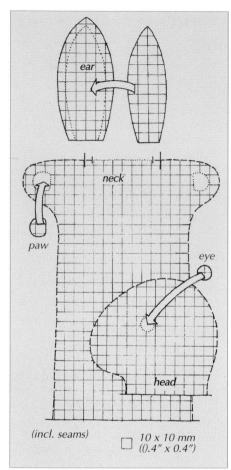

Figure 22-1. Pattern for glove puppet.

• Sew up the sides and sew the ears on to the head in such a way that the seam is at the back.

• For the rucksack cast on 16 stitches and knit 8 rows plain. Run the stitches on to the knitting yarn, pull the yarn tight and break off.

• Sew the rucksack on to the back, securing the yarn crosswise with a few stitches to make the rucksack-straps.

• Embroider a nose, give the hare some side-whiskers and sew the beads in place for eyes (Figure 22-2).

• Finally place a small egg in the rucksack.

An Easter hare as a glove puppet

❖ *Pieces of fabric, preferably knitted cotton for the body*
Pieces of pink felt for the inside of the ears and paws
Brown felt for the eyes
Unspun sheep's wool
Embroidery-thread

• Select a suitable piece of the material and cut out head, body and the ears each twice (Figure 22-1).

• First sew the pink front on to the ears. Sew the sides together inside out and turn them. The bottom is thus still open.

• Sew the eyes on to the separate halves of the head. Sew the halves inside out on to each other leaving the neck open. Turn the right side out.

• Then embroider the pink inside of the paws on to the two pieces of the body. Sew together the two halves of the body inside-out leaving the bottom and the neck open. Turn the body right side out, and hem the bottom.

• Now all the separate pieces can be sewn together. First sew the head into the neck of the body and then the ears on to the head.

• Finish off the Easter hare by filling the head with some unspun wool and make a hole in the wool with your finger so that later a finger will fit in when the hare is played with. Finally give the animal an embroidered nose and side-whiskers.

Figure 22-2. Finger puppets.

Figure 22-3. Glove puppet.

Figure 22-4. Egg decorated by children.

5 Decorating Easter Eggs

Decorating eggs is a custom which goes back to before the beginnings of recorded history. The egg was seen as the symbol for germinating power and new life.

There are many ways of decorating Easter eggs. The method depends on what you want to do with the eggs. Are they going to be eaten or just used for decoration?

If they are to be eaten we can decorate boiled egg before they come on to the Easter breakfast table or are hidden in the garden. The decoration is short-lived and for once only.

For decoration a blown-out egg can be hung on an Easter tree or blossoming branch, for the whole time from Easter to Ascension. You can even keep blown-out eggs carefully for another year.

For some of the methods, for example with batik, you will have to immerse the egg in a liquid. This is not really suitable for blown-out eggs, and is better used for eggs which have been very hard boiled (half an hour or more), so that they don't spoil so quickly.

Before beginning to decorate

The quality of the eggshell can differ greatly; so check whether it is too thin (it can crack or break while it is being boiled or blown out) and check whether the surface is nice and smooth.

White eggs are the best for decorating but they are often hard to obtain.
● Eggshells are always a bit greasy. To enable the paint or colouring to stick properly the grease should first be removed from the egg with some vinegar or washing-up liquid.
● Make a hole in the top and bottom of the egg with a pin or an egg-pricker.
● These holes are still too small to let you blow the egg out, so take two large round nails, one about 2 mm ($^1/_{12}$") thick and the other about 4 mm ($^1/_5$") thick. Sharpen the points of the nails so that they can serve as a kind of drill.
● Make one of the holes in the egg just a little larger (the hole you blow through) and use the thin nail at the other end to make the hole bigger (Figure 23-1).
● Blow the egg out over a jar (use it for scrambled eggs or omelettes), then rinse out the inside of the eggshell a little by letting some water flow in through the hole and blowing it out again, or by taking some water into your mouth and blowing it through the egg. This is to ensure that no residue is left in the shell.
● Make sure that no water remains in the shell to avoid problems while you are painting the egg.
● Figure 23-2 shows a very simple gadget, Blas-fix, which makes the blowing-out of eggs much easier, by only requiring one hole and no blowing.

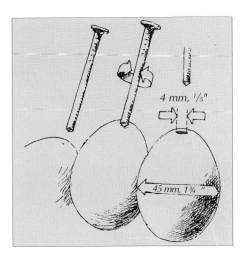

Figure 23-1. Making holes in the egg.

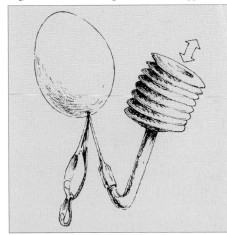

Figure 23-2. A Blas-fix.

Batik variation
When eggs have to be left for some time submerged in a bath of hot dye, make the larger hole bigger with the thicker nail. This is done by twisting the nail slowly round applying light pressure: the sharp edges cut into the egg without breaking it. The dye can now enter the eggshell and it stays submerged.

Hanging up the eggs

① After the egg is decorated tie the end of a length of thread firmly around the middle of half a match-stick (or wire) and poke the match with the thread through the hole in the egg. Now pull the thread carefully and the match will come to rest across the hole and will not come out any more.

② If the egg has two slightly larger holes you can run a thin ribbon right through the egg and tie a bow in it at the bottom of the egg.

● Now the egg can be hung up.

< *Figure 24-1.*

Figure 25-1. Methods of hanging eggs.

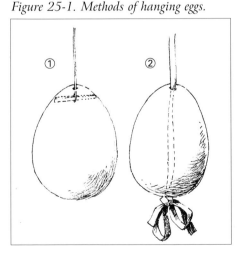

Eggs to be decorated by children

❖ *Coloured pencils or*
  Wax crayons

Decorating eggs with coloured pencils or wax crayons is very simple (Figure 22-4). For children thick crayons or block-crayons are best. Even the smallest children can take part.

Note that blown-out eggs are very fragile and can easily be squashed by young children. Hard boiled eggs are more suitable.

Colouring eggs with plant dyes

❖ *Tea, coffee, camomile, onion skin, juice from spinach, beetroot and so on.*

Everyday plant-products used in the kitchen are suitable for dying eggs, such as tea-leaves, coffee, camomile and onion skin, or vegetables like spinach and beetroot. Exotic plants and insect-dyes such as tumeric from India sandalwood from Africa, or cochineal from the West Indies will also produce very beautiful colours. Some of these products are sold as egg-dyes. In general they need only a short time on the boil (see also "Materials" on page 116).

● Put the material to make the dye into a pot of cold water and bring to a boil. Then carefully immerse the thoroughly cleaned egg into the boiling water. Of course white eggs will take on better colours than brown eggs.

● With some materials, like coffee and tea, first bring the water to boiling before adding the material. Leave to boil for a short time before immersing the eggs.

● You will have to experiment a bit first especially with the length of time for boiling.

● Plant dyes cannot be used indefinitely. After five or six eggs have been boiled in them the colour begins to fade. Use a small saucepan and make sure that the eggs are fully immersed, or turn them over regularly.

You can get a whole range of colours. They can be made more intense by a dash of vinegar.

— *light yellow:* camomile flowers, marigold petals
— *light brown:* onion skin (five to ten minutes)
— *dark brown:* strong black tea or coffee
— *red:* beetroot juice is very good, pokeberries
— *green:* boiled liquid of spinach or nettles
— *violet:* huckleberries, grapes

● Once the eggs have dried off thoroughly after their colour-bath they can be rubbed with a cloth dipped in salad oil. This will give them a soft sheen and the colour will not rub off so easily.

The eggs on the Easter tree in Figure 14-1 were coloured with plant dyes.

Painting eggs with water-colours

❖ *Paints (water-colours, poster colours or plant dyes)*
  Paint brushes
  Wooden barbecue sticks or thin knitting needles
  A piece of wire
  A little modelling wax

One of the difficulties of painting an egg with water-colours (artists or poster) is how to hold it so that you

Figure 26-1. Colours scratched away.

Figure 26-2. Stamped eggs.

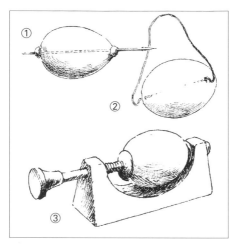

Figure 26-3.

don't put your fingers on the wet painted part, and yet being able to keep turning the egg round as you paint. There are several ways of overcoming this difficulty.

① One simple way is to push a long wooden barbecue stick (or thin knitting needle) through both holes and secure it with a bit of modelling wax.

② Another way is to bend a bit of wire so that it acts as a pair of tongs with each end of the wire inserted in the holes of the egg.

③ Finally there are egg-holders on the market which hold the egg. The holder comes with six different watercolours made of natural substances, which are safe for young children.

• You can simply paint the egg or first put it into a colour-bath to provide a background colour. Use the paint fairly thickly. If it is too thin, it will run on the round, non-porous surface of the egg.

• Once the eggs are thoroughly dry apply a coat of varnish so that the colours will not subsequently run.

Eggs with decorating wax

❖ *Blocks of modelling wax in various colours*
Strips of decorating wax in various colours
A sharp knife or skewer

• Take a small piece of modelling wax and warm it by kneading it a bit. When the wax has become soft apply it thinly to the egg pressing it on firmly. Cut out the shape with a knife or skewer.
• You can pare off very thin strips of decorating wax with a knife. Apply them carefully to the egg and press on firmly. Because the wax is transparent you can apply several layers of different colours over each other (Figure 24-1).

Decorating eggs by scratching away the colour

❖ *A sharp craft-knife*

• For this scratching-away technique it is important that the egg should have a strong shell. Of course you can also scratch out designs on hard-boiled eggs.
• Start with a strongly coloured egg and first sketch the designs with a fine pencil.
• Now take a sharp craft-knife. Scrape away several times to remove the colour completely and allow the plain white eggshell to become visible.
• By not removing all the colour you will leave a lighter shade (Figure 26-1).

Potato stamping eggs

❖ *Poster paints*
A raw potato
A kitchen knife

By using a stamp you can keep repeating the same design so that you get a symmetrical effect. By using different colours and by turning the egg you can achieve interesting effects (Figure 26-2).
① Cut a potato into several large pieces, each of them having one flat surface. Dry the potato with kitchen paper.
② ③ With a knife carve out a design in the flat surface and use the potato as a stamp (Figure 27-1).
• Squeeze out some undiluted poster paint on to a flat surface, press the stamp into it and print on to the egg. Continue round the egg. If desired use different colours.
• Allow the paint to dry thoroughly and coat with varnish.

Decorating eggs with trimmings and wool

❖ *Fabric trimmings*
Glue
Different coloured wools
A glue-stick

Figure 28-1 shows how you can make a very simple decoration with fabric trimmings. Just stick trimmings on to the egg with glue. Use a quick-drying glue with a fine nozzle so that not too much glue comes on to the egg. Surplus glue makes unwanted shiny patches when dry.
• Begin by using a gluestick: apply a little glue to the top (or bottom) making sure that you leave the hole open.
① Press one end of the yarn into the glue and make a nice round loop. Press the loop well down and run the yarn carefully round the loop, applying a little glue as you go till you have gone round once or twice.
② When changing colour, lay the new colour against the old one and run the yarn round the egg once. Pass the second colour over the yarn of the first,

Figure 27-1. Making a potato stamp.

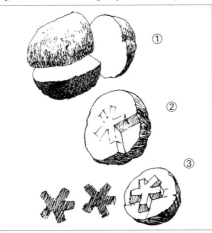

Figure 27-2. Gluing woollen yarn.

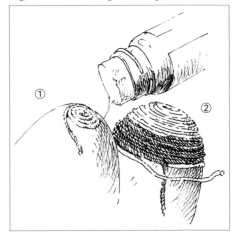

leaving the yarn of the first colour to hang down — which can be taken up again later. Always start the new colours at the same place.

• To obtain a symmetrically decorated egg stick the yarns on alternately at the top and at the bottom until they meet in the middle.

• Cut off the loose hanging yarns when the egg is finished and stick the cut-off ends firmly on to the egg.

Decorating eggs with dried flowers and leaves

❖ *Dried flowers or leaves*
  Glue

At Easter time there are hardly any flowers suitable for drying. Ideally use a flower-press during the previous summer to make a collection of dried flowers for Easter (see page 41).

• As an egg is only about 6 cm (2½") high, use small flowers and leaves for decorating it.

• Select those flowers, flower-clusters and leaves which have strong silhouette forms or which are very regular in shape. A wreath of leaves round a stem can be very effective, also a highly indented leaf can look very good on an egg. Thin petals are easily torn when being stuck on to the egg.

• Stick the flowers and leaves on to white or coloured eggs with a bit of glue. After gluing press the flowers and leaves flat with your hand and hold them in position until the glue dries (Figure 31-2).

< *Figure 28-1.*

Decorating eggs with quilling

❖ *Quilling paper*
  Quilling-pen
  Tweezers
  Tube of adhesive with a fine nozzle

Working with quilling paper is delicate work but it gives a lot of pleasure and the coloured rolls of paper can look very effective.

Quilling-paper work is an ancient craft using narrow strips of paper wound round the quill of a goose feather. A little slit was made in the end of the quill into which one end of the strip of paper was fitted.

• Use strips of paper 3–4 mm (⅛") wide. They usually come in lengths of 50 cm (20"). Decide whether to take a half or a quarter length for your work.

• Instead of the real quill of a goose-feather there are quilling-pens available. One end of the quilling paper is inserted in the slit of the quill and the strip is now wound round the quilling-pen. Instead of a quilling-pen you can use a cocktail-stick. If you are expert in this technique you can even use a pin, for the smaller the hole inside the better the result will be.

• Once the strip has been wound right round the quill finish off by sticking the end down with glue. As soon as you take the roll off the quill or cocktail-stick, the strip will roll out to the stuck-on end so that you will get this particular effect.

Figure 29-1.

• With an open spiral it is not necessary to do the sticking. The blue spirals in Figure 31-4 and 31-7 shows these. With the little rolls in the illustration the end has been stuck down without the loop. Of course there are plenty of variations and other forms possible.

Decorating eggs with straw and wood-shavings

❖ *Craft straws*
  Rolls of shavings
  A pair of tweezers
  A sharp knife of pair of scissors
  Glue
  A piece of zinc or perspex as a cutting board

Working with straw or shavings is a delicate job. The bits are often so tiny that you need tweezers to hold them.

Wood shavings are very pliable and thin and so easy to work.

Straw by contrast is much stiffer but has a shining surface: it must be steeped in water for half an hour before it can be split open and ironed flat. It is better to do this part of the work the day before and to press the ironed straw in a book to prevent it from curling.

The eggs in Figures 31-5 and 31-6 are decorated with straws while Figures 31-8 and 31-9 show eggs decorated with wood shavings.

• On a piece of paper draw the oval shape of an egg and make a sketch of the design which you wish to make. This entails quite a bit of experimentation.

- Working with straw is more satisfying with symmetrical designs. Cut out the desired figures in their final shape and lay them out ready.
- If you find it difficult to stick the desired shape straight on to the egg you can first trace a few faint guiding lines on the egg with a sharp pencil.
- Now start to stick the shapes on, using the tweezers if necessary. Apply adhesive with a fine nozzle so that your work is as neat as possible.
- From time to time press the bits carefully on with your hand. As the egg progresses you can see whether the design requires any more to be added or even some parts to be left bare. Begin with simple designs, and only try more complex ones when you have built up some experience.
- The pink egg in Figure 31-9 is plastered with squares. Such a design is difficult because squares and a round egg don't belong together. Make the front and back the same, and fiddle the sides a bit (as can be seen on the lower edge of the picture).

Making batik eggs with flowers and plants

❖ *Dry brown onion skin*
Young leaves and flowers
Old nylon stockings
Thread

- Take one or more simple little flowers or leaves, wet them and lay them on the unboiled egg. As long as they are damp they will stay in place.
- Take as big an onion skin as possible and cover the leaf and the egg with it. Then wrap the egg in a number of onion skins until you cannot see anything more of the egg. Put the whole thing into a nylon stocking and tie this up tightly round the egg so that the onion skins stay in place.
- Make a bed of onion skins in a saucepan with water, and lay the egg in the nylon stocking on the bed. Fill the saucepan with water, bring to a boil, and leave it all to boil for about ten minutes.
- Allow the egg to cool off in the saucepan before taking it out of its wrapping. When the last onion skin and the leaves have been removed you will see that the egg has a brown colour while the shape of the leaves has been left.
- To give the eggs a soft sheen you can rub them lightly with salad oil.
- Alternatively the eggs can be died with textile dyes suitable for cold baths.

Czech and Ukrainian batik eggs

Decorating eggs with batik is an ancient folk-art in Slavic countries which is still practised today. There are significant differences in form and motif according to each country or region. The two eggs at the top of Figure 32-1 are Czech, and their main motifs are sun and flowers. The two eggs at the bottom of the Figure come from the Ukraine, where geometrical forms are more common.

❖ *Beeswax (thinned with paraffin if required)*
A candle
A tjanting (kiska) or holder with a nail
Vinegar
A flannel cloth
Elastic bands
Batik dyes

This method requires much patience and practice; in the beginning you can expect things to go wrong! It is best to start with very simple designs. Figure 33-1 shows a number of basic forms which of course can be developed further.

You can use both hard-boiled and blown-out eggs; the heavier boiled egg is easier to submerge in the dye-bath.

- Rub the egg clean with a cloth dipped in vinegar (to remove any remains of grease). After that always hold the egg with a cloth, as any grease from your hand will prevent the egg from taking on the dye.

① The simplest *batik-pen* is a round wooden stick with a nail stuck in it. This was used to make the patterns in this book.
② You can also get a tjanting or kiska, which has a nozzle with a brass

Figure 31-1.

Figure 31-2.

Figure 31-3.

Figure 31-4.

Figure 31-5.

Figure 31-6.

√ *Figure 31-7.*

√ *Figure 31-8.*

√ *Figure 31-9.*

31

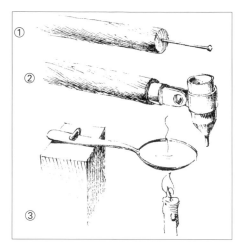

Figure 32-2.

container for the liquid wax. Tjantings for cloth-batik have a much smaller nozzle. By heating the container above a candle flame the wax will remain liquid.

- There is also a batik-pen the point of which you hold in a candle flame until it is well heated and then you dip it into a block of beeswax which produces a thin layer of liquid wax around the pen.
- Finally you can apply the wax with the quill of a feather; the shape of the quill will determine the character of the design.

- Heat the beeswax in a tin placed in a pan of boiling water (this prevents the wax boiling excessively). If the wax is not runny enough, thin it with a little paraffin.
③ Use an old spoon over a candle as a wax reservoir.
- Applying the wax is a tricky job. You have to keep dipping the point of the nail into the liquid wax as you draw on the egg with the wax.
- Aesthetically, an egg demands symmetry. Always begin the floral patterns in the middle and work your way outwards (see the top egg in Figure 32-1).

The same applies when you are making bands or festoons.
- To start it can be a help to draw the design on the egg very lightly with a yellow or blue coloured pencil. Before you make lines or festoons which go right round the egg you can slip one or two elastic bands round the egg as a marker.
- Remember the areas covered in wax will remain white, while the uncovered areas will take on the colour.
- Begin by making an egg with a single colour only, draw the design on the egg with the wax pen. The wax will dry almost immediately.
- The egg can now be immersed in the dye-bath. The dye liquid must be cold otherwise the wax will melt. Keep the egg immersed until it has acquired the right intensity of colour. When you remove the egg from the dye you will see that the wax of the design has prevented the dye from colouring the egg there, so now you have a white design on the colour background.
- It is difficult to immerse a blown-out egg. You can run a stick or thin knitting needle through the egg (Figure 26-3 ①) and pour the dye over the egg.
- Warm the egg in the oven or with a hair-dryer until the wax begins to melt, when it can be wiped with paper tissues, leaving a thin protective layer on the egg.
- You can also rub in a little oil, and the egg is finished.

- To do batik eggs with several colours begin with the lightest colour. With the batik-pen draw a design on the white egg and immerse the egg in the dye-bath, for example in yellow.
- If the wax were now to be removed you would get a white drawing on a yellow background (as described above); but now leave the wax on, and once the colour has dried make a fresh design, this time on the yellow background.

Figure 32-1. Batik eggs.

- Now choose a darker dye-bath, red for example. The result is a drawing in white and a drawing in yellow on a red background.
- Make a new design on the red background and immerse the egg in a still darker dye-bath, black for example. When the egg is removed after that, and the melting wax wiped away a design emerges on the egg in white, yellow and red on a black background.

6 Working with Paper

Simple transparencies

Chapter 16 on page 76 describes many different kinds of transparencies from simple to more complicated ones.

Cutting out concertina paper

❖ *Thin card (about 150 gsm, 40 lb bond) in various colours*
A sharp knife or a pointed pair of scissors
Glue

There are many suitable subjects. Here we describe an Easter hare, a chicken and a cockerel.
- Don't take too thick a card and don't make too many folds because you will not be able to cut through the thickness.
- First look at the size of the card and how often it can be folded. If you have an even number of panels, this will give symmetry.

① Cut out a strip of card and fold concertina fashion.
② Sketch out the required shapes on a piece of paper. Then copy this design on to the outside of the card or trace the design with carbon paper.
- It is important that there is enough contact between the figures at the folds otherwise the finished cut-out will fall over.
③ Cut out the figures with scissors or a sharp knife. The cut-out can still be decorated or coloured by the children.

- It is also an idea to cut out two or more designs and set them up in front of each other to make a kind of story as in Figure 34-2 where the hen comes running up to the cock.

Figure 33-1. Basic patterns for batik.

Figure 33-2.

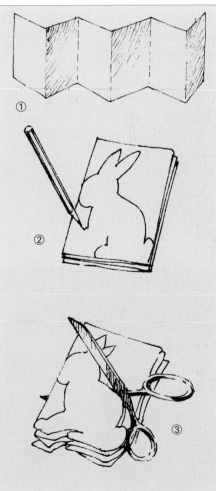

Figure 34-1. Concertina Easter hare.

Figure 34-2. Concertina chickens.

∨*Figure 34-3. Concertina chickens.*

An origami chicken

❖ *A number of square sheets for folding of a colour of your own choice (about 10 cm, 4" square)*
  A piece of orange or red cardboard
  Glue

① Fold the sheet once across the diagonal so that point B comes on to point C and open it again.
② Now fold points B and C to the middle to the diagonal and stick them down with a tiny bit of glue.
③ Then fold point D to point A.
④ Turn the piece round so that points E and F are interchanged and make a vertical fold through A so that point E comes on to point F.
⑤ Draw corners A and D apart and make a new fold.
⑥ Press point A inwards so that you make a beak. Cut out a comb from bit of cardboard and stick it in the fold which you have just made.
● Now the chicken can stand on the new fold. If we make fold *b* a bit smaller and fold *a* bit bigger the chicken will stand on fold-line *a* and look as if she is pecking.
● You can also give the chicken eyes.
● Sheets of different sizes will result in a flock of different-sized chicks.

middle to the diagonal and stick them together with a tiny bit of glue.
③ Fold E and F also to the diagonal and stick them with a tiny bit of glue.
④ Fold the piece over along the diagonal so that points E and F come to the outside as shown. Cut into the line BC from B a quarter of the total length BC and from C up to point E. Then cut into the line EG about half the distance EG.

Figure 35-1. Origami chicken.

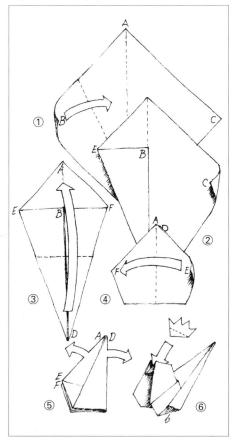

An origami hare

❖ *Sheets of colour of your own choice, size for example 14 × 14 cm (5½" × 5½")*
  Glue

① Fold the sheet once across the diagonal so that point A comes over point D. Open again.② Fold A and D to the

Figure 35-2. Origami chicken.

Figure 35-3. Origami hare.

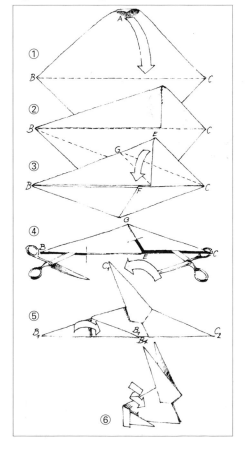

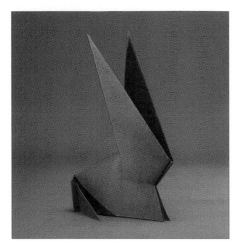

Figure 36-1. Origami hare.

is about a quarter of the fold along which it is folded.
④ Fold E and F to each other so that the point D which has just been folded comes to the outside.
• Work the point of D to the front, press the fold which you have thus made firmly and your swan is finished.

Figure 36-2. Origami swan.

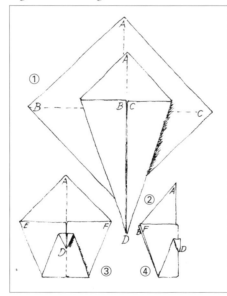

⑤ This makes two points C and two points B. The Figure shows how point C_1 is folded upwards to make one of the two ears, while B_1 is folded forward to make one of the hindlegs. Repeat with C_2 and B_2.
⑥ Make an extra fold at the hindlegs to emphasise them and to enable the hare to stand better.
• Then you can let the children colour the hare with crayons.
• Here too you can vary the size of the sheets.

An origami swan

❖ *White sheets 12 × 12 cm (4¾" × 4¾")*
Glue

① Fold the sheet once across the diagonal so that point B comes over point C. Open again.
② Fold B and C in to the diagonal.
③ Fold point D up to where points B and C come together.
• Fold D back so that the folded point

Figure 36-3. Origami swan.

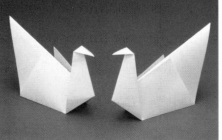

7 Summer

Whitsun bird made of dough

• Make a dough as in the recipe on page 17. Divide the dough into eight portions.
• Roll out each portion to a long strip and tie a knot in it. Make a few cuts into the tail.
• With a knife make a hole for the eye and one for the beak. You can put a raisin in for the eye and a nut for the beak.

Figure 36-4. Whitsun bird.

Tissue-paper butterflies

❖ *Sheets of tissue-paper of various colours*
Wooden barbecue sticks
Poster paints
Modelling wax
Thin wire
Glue

• For each butterfly select three different colours of tissue-paper. Cut out a sheet 8 × 9 cm (3" × 3½") and fold it in two so that you get the size 8 × 4.5 cm (3" × 1¾"). Draw the shape of one half of the wings of a butterfly and cut this out. Repeat this with the other two sheets.

• Indicate with a pencil how much smaller the second set of wings must be and cut them out. Repeat with the third set of wings.

• Stick the wings together in the fold with a little bit of glue. Make the "eyes" of the butterfly out of a scrap of tissue-paper and stick them on.

• Take a wooden barbecue stick and paint it. Fold a piece of thin wire in two. Twist the doubled end round the end of the skewer and cover this with a blob of brown modelling wax. If necessary you can cut the ends of the wire to the right length and press a little blob of wax on to the two ends.

• Finally stick the wings firmly on to the barbecue stick. Put the butterfly in a pot with flowers (Figure 37-2).

Little doves of cardboard and tissue-paper

❖ *Thin white card (about 145 gsm)*
White tissue-paper or tracing paper
A pair of scissors with a sharp point
Thread

① On the cardboard first draw the head, body and tail of the dove and then cut them out. Cut out or draw the eye. Make a slot in the middle of the body to take the wings.

② For the wings take a piece of tissue-paper or tracing paper 12 × 8 cm (4¾" × 3¼"). Mark 12 equal divisions along the long side, and fold the paper concertina fashion twelve times.

③ Push these folded-up strips into the slot in the dove's body. Fold the two ends upwards and stick them together with a little bit of glue.

• Insert a thread (with a needle) in the edge of the bird to hang it up by. The Figure shows a mobile with twelve doves.

Figure 37-1.

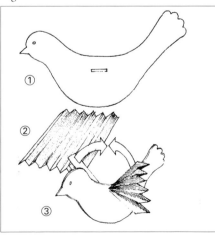

∧ *Figures 37-2.*   *Figure 37-3.* ∨

Flowers made of tissue-paper

❖ *Various colours of tissue-paper*
Copper wire (0.8 mm, $^1/_{32}$" thick)
Glue
A wad of cotton-wool
Stout thread
A small pointed pair of pliers
Very thin wire (0.25–0.35 mm, $^1/_{64}$")

The stalk and the heart

The picture opposite shows a vase with a number of different flowers which can be made in three different ways. You can copy real flowers as exactly as possible, or you can freely use your imagination.

① The stalk is the same for all these flowers. Take a piece of copper or steel wire (copper wire is more pliable). The length depends on the size of the vase you are going to use.

② Using pliers, make a kind of a curl at one end of the wire round which you put a piece of cotton-wool. Lay it on a square piece of tissue-paper. The colour of the tissue-paper depends on the colour of the rest of the flower.

③ Fold the tissue-paper over the cotton-wool and secure it underneath.

④ For flowers with stamens in their hearts take a few pieces of very thin wire about 6–7 cm (2½") long and tie a bead on to the end of each wire. Join the stamens to each other by twisting the wires together. Attach this bundle on to the thicker wire by winding it round a loop a few times.

⑤ For flowers like the rose which have no visible heart, take a piece of wire and bend over one end. Stick a bit of tissue-paper over this end. This will give you a better hold when it comes to winding on the flower.

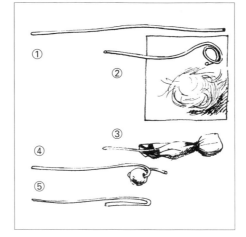
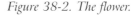

Figure 38-1. Stalk and heart.

The basic flower

① Choose a colour for the petals and cut out a strip from a sheet of tissue-paper of this colour. The length (for the height of flower) can be 4–5 cm (1½"–2").

② Fold the long strip in two and then again and so on until you come down to the required width of the petal. This width can vary from 4 cm (1½") for red and pink roses to 2 cm (¾") for dark yellow flowers.

③ Cut one end of the folded pack into a round form.

• Unfold the pack. Stick one end of the strip to the top of the stalk with a bit of glue. If you stick the strip on too low down you may find that when you come to wind on the petals, they stick too close together.

• Begin by rucking the petals together at the bottom and at the same time wind the strip round the wire, going progressively lower.

• Once the strip has been fully wound round the wire stick down the end. Check whether the flower is filled out enough. If not, repeat the process with a half or possibly a whole strip.

• Tie up the bottom of the petals with a bit of thread and finish off the stalk by wrapping a strip of green tissue-paper round the wire.

• Cut out the leaves. Stick them onto the stalk, making sure they are firmly glued at the bottom.

Figure 39-1. >

Figure 38-2. The flower.

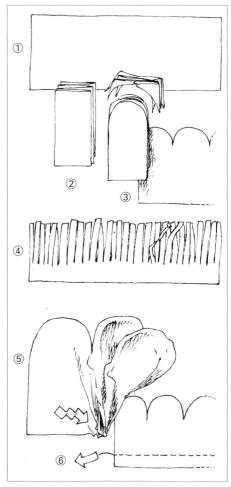

Carnations
- To make carnation-like flowers with petals consisting of very small strips, keep on folding the cut-out strip until you have the width of a petal, but remember that your scissors must be able to cut through the thickness of the pack.
④ Make cuts close together into one side. Finish as described above.

Six-petalled flowers
In Figure 39-1 the yellow flower sticking out above to the right has six petals. Depending on the size of the flower the petals have a width of about 2–4 cm (1"–1½").
- Select three, four or five different or the same colours of tissue-paper. Follow steps ① ② and ③ in Figure 382.
- Cut out the strips and lay them on top of each other before you begin to fold them.
- Lay the three, four or five strips on top of each other and concertina fold six petals. After cutting out the petals roundly all the strips will be have the same pattern.

⑤ Unfold the strips and stick them on to each other at the bottom so that they overlap.
⑥ Run a thread through all the petals one third up from the bottom. With this tacking thread the strips are now tied together, so now you can cut off the bottoms about 5 mm (¼") from the thread.

- Stick the top and bottom petals together to make a round cylinder with a little strip of tissue-paper of the right colour. Instead of sticking a strip on two petals you can of course anticipate this by leaving a little strip on one of the ends when you cut it.
- Pull in the threads as tightly as possible and tie up the ends. Push the stalk through it and stick the pistil on to the petals. Open out the petals nicely.
- For the rest finish off the flower in the same way as the basic flower.

Flowers with separate petals
- Fold a strip of tissue-paper into a pack cut out the separate petals.

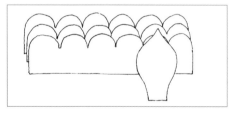

Figure 40-1

- Stick the petals on one by one onto the paper under the pistil (which has already been tied on). Each successive petal comes a little bit further up to overlap. Choose the number and colours of petals.
- Once the last petal has been stuck on, secure them with a thread and they will splay out by themselves. If necessary tug out one or other petal a bit more.
- The rest of the finishing off is as in the basic flower described above.

Elves made of tissue-paper

❖ *Tissue-paper of different colours*
Sewing thread of different colours
Unspun wool or cotton-wool
A piece of thick wire or cane for the hoop

- On a sheet of blank paper draw a circle with a radius of about 7 cm (2¾"). Then draw the wings (Figure 41-1). Cut out the two drawings.
- Lay the cut-out patterns of the elf and the wings on a sheet of tissue-paper and cut out the two shapes. Using the patterns cut out the desired number of elves.
- Make a little ball of the unspun wool or cotton-wool about the size of the tip of your little finger. Lay the ball in the middle of the round piece of tissue-paper, fold one half over and make sure that the ball stays well in the middle to make the head. Tie a piece of similar coloured sewing-thread round the neck.
- See which side is the best and make it the front. If the knot in the thread lands unexpectedly to the front, tie another knot at the back. Make sure that both ends of the thread are still long enough.

Figure 40-2. Elves made of tissue-paper.

- With these ends tie the wings firmly on to the middle of the back. Pull in the threads tight so that the wings don't wobble. Cut off the ends of the threads.
- Take a fresh thread of the same colour and push it through the neck of the elf with a needle so that a thread comes out on each side of the head. Tie both threads about 4 cm (1½") above the head.
- Cut off one of the threads and use the other to hang the elf up. You can now add a drape of tissue paper for a cloak.
- Make a hoop of wire or piece of cane, wind coloured tissue-paper around it and hang the elves from it.

Drying flowers

Throughout the year you can find various flowers to dry — for instance roses, thistles, daisies and so on. Hang them in a dark, dry place by the stalk. Don't leave them in vase until they have almost died, but to hang them up well before they wilt.

A leaf and flower-press

❖ *Two plywood boards 20 × 20 cm (8" × 8") and 8 mm (³/₈") thick*
  6–8 pieces of corrugated cardboard 20 × 20 cm (8" × 8")
  A number of sheets of tissue-paper 20 × 20 cm (8" × 8")
  4 bolts, 4–6 cm (2") long, 6 mm (¼") diameter (No 14), with wing-nuts and washers

- Sandpaper the plywood boards. Draw the two diagonals to find the right place to make the holes, which should be about 2–3 cm (1") from the corners.
- Press the bolts through the holes of one of the boards, hammering them in tight if necessary. Cut off the corners of the corrugated cardboard and the tissue-papers so that they fit inside the bolts of the boards. Lay a few sheets of tissue-paper between each layer of cardboard.
- Lay the other board on top, fit the washers and tighten the nuts.
- You can decorate the wooden boards of the flower-press with crayon or water-colours.

- To dry and press flowers and leaves to be stored, lay them between two sheets of tissue-paper to ensure that any special features are preserved.
- If any parts of the flower should be too thick, such as a root, a stalk, a twig or the beginning of the fruit, carefully cut away the parts which are too thick with a sharp knife, or even cut the stalk in half.
- The flowers should be kept in the press for a few weeks in order to dry out thoroughly.

Figure 41-1.

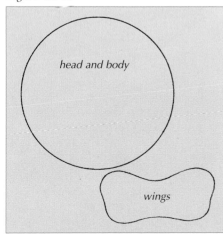

Figure 41-2.

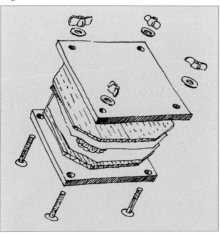

8 Working with Straw

From the time when grain became food for Humankind, after the harvest had been gathered in, the harvesters would make from the last sheaf of corn a harvest symbol which was then offered to the gods as thanksgiving for an abundant harvest and as a prayer for a new fruitful year. Thus for example in ancient Egypt the straw was made into a doll, the *grain-mother*.

Through the centuries the form of this grain-mother or straw-doll changed, and so with the coming of Christianity there came the harvest-cross, which at the end of the harvest was borne to the church (see Figure 46-3).

Right up to the beginning of this century many plaited symbols were made in England (and also in other places in Europe); among them there are those known as "corn-dollies."

With combine-harvesters, which thresh the corn and bale the straw at the same time, the custom of making a doll from the last sheaf has lapsed, and with it the skill of plaiting straw has also vanished. Some straw decorations described here are based on traditional motifs, others are new designs.

❖ *A pair of garden clippers or old scissors (straw is really hard and scissors soon become blunt)*
  A pair of scissors with sharp points (for finishing off)
  A kitchen knife (for removing thin leaves from the stem)
  Thin string or stout thread (button-thread) in natural colours
  Thick needles
  A tape-measure

The length of the plait and the number of straws required is given as a guide for every pattern. Obviously, this can be varied.

Straw decorations

For making autumn decorations from straw and ears of corn wheat or rye ears work best. Wheat-straw is generally the easiest to use as it is fairly pliant.

Depending on the weather, harvesting takes place in July or August, ask the farmer for straw or whole ears just before the corn is cut. See that the corn is not too near a highway, for the grain can be rather grey and dirty.

Sometimes you can find some ears still standing along the edge of the corn-field after the cutting, or the harvester has left some cut corn which has not been threshed. For convenience this will be called "waste straw." Wind and rain will often rob it of its golden-yellow lustre leaving it a greenish colour. Even though the stalks are often broken and flattened they are still quite usable. The models of Figures 45-2, 3 and 4 are made of this waste straw. Finally of course you can grow your own corn in a sunny patch of your garden.

You don't always need stalks *with* ears, which can be cut off at the first nodule. If, however, the *whole stalk* is required see that the ear stands up nicely.

Wheat with its chaff-husks has a beautiful form.

Barley ears have grains in two rows which give a characteristic effect.

The light, airy **oat** is generally used only for decoration.

The colour of the ears is partly determined by the composition of the soil on which it grows. Soil containing iron can give a reddish-brown ear.

The Stalks

The stalk consists of a long stem with nodules at regular intervals. Out of these nodules grow long narrow leaves which are wrapped round the stalk. The stalk is thicker at the bottom than up at the ear — becoming thinner at each nodule.

The further apart the nodules the better the stalk is suited for plaiting, for the nodules are tough and cannot be bent easily. If the stalks are very thick at the bottom and very thin at the top then it is best to use only the middle part of the stalk, for the lower part is then often too hard to plait, and the top looks too thin.

The straws are best stored by binding them together with an elastic band and hanging the bunch upside down (reducing the chance of breaking the ears).

The length of the straws depends on the type of grain, where it grows, the humidity and the temperature in the springtime. The length to be used will be determined by the kind of work to be done.

A bouquet of various cereals

❖ *A basket*
  Oasis (florist's flower block)
  A knife
  Various kinds of cereals: oat, wheat, rye and barley

① Cut out a good piece of the oasis measured so that it fits neatly into the basket, leaving about 1.5–2 cm (¾") above the rim.
② Imagine or lightly draw a triangle A_1–A_2–A_3 on to the surface of the oasis. Push three ears of the same kind obliquely into the rim of the oasis below each point.
③ Now imagine or lightly draw a second triangle B_1–B_2–B_3, and insert an ear of another kind into the oasis below each of these points. Repeat this with a third triangle, C_1–C_2–C_3. Make sure that all the ears are of the same length so that the basket, when made up, will be nice and round.

• Push a good ear of wheat or rye into the centre of the oasis. You can insert another three ears obliquely a little away from the centre of the oasis.
④ Fill the whole piece of oasis *lightly* with oat-ears 8–10 cm (3"–4") high. This grain is softer and hides the oasis.

• Begin inserting the remaining ears towards the middle, working from below up and going round all the time. Ears which are hanging down should of course be facing outwards.

Preparations for plaiting

• Before the straws are worked they must be *peeled*, that is to say the long thin leaves which often lie closely round the stalk must be removed. This is best done by running a potato-peeler down the stalk from top to bottom. This must be done carefully otherwise the stalk can break at the nodules (Figure 43-2). Make sure that the leaves are completely removed round the nodules.

Figure 43-1.

• By nature, dry straws are stiff and not pliable, so that before plaiting they must be soaked. Lay them in a bath or tub with warm water for an hour, weighing them down with a pail or plate so that they lie well covered with water (Figure 43-3). Only freshly-cut stalks are still pliant enough to be plaited without being first soaked.

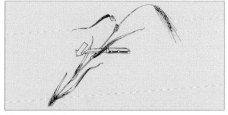

Figure 43-2.

∧ *Figures 43-3.*   *Figure 43-4.* ∨

- Don't leave the straws in the water for too long, as this will affect their quality adversely. So don't soak any more straws than you require for plaiting. You will need some practice before being able to judge how much straw you will need for any particular article. Depending on the thickness and tightness of the plait, it will be 50% to 60% of the length of the flat straws, so that for each plait you will need two or three times its length of straws.

Plaiting a straw heart

❖ *Waste straw*
   Length: c. 66 cm (26")

- Use straws *without* ears. Take them out of the water first cutting off any bits too thin and any nodules at the end of the straws. Although there are various methods of plaiting only the simplest with three straws will be used in this book.

- For the straw hearts on page 45 begin with twelve or fifteen straws depending on their thickness. As straws are thinner at the top, turn some of the straws round so that the thickness of the bundle remains even (Figure 44-1).

① To get as tight a plait as possible tie the end of the bundle of straws firmly together with string.

② For this a *clove-hitch* is a handy knot as it can be drawn tight immediately. Then tie an extra knot if necessary. In order to plait tightly tie the other end of the string to something.

③ For plaiting you can use a *plaiting-board*. This is a board about 25 × 80 cm (10" × 32") which has four nails driven in at one end. As the plaiting proceeds the string can be wound round the nails so that the actual point of plaiting remains at the same distance from your body.

① Divide the bundle of straws into three equal parts (Figure 44-2).

② First the bundle of straws furthest to the right (C) is brought over the bundle in the middle (B).

③ Then bring the left-hand bundle (A) over bundle (C) which has now become the middle bundle.

④ Then bring the right-hand bundle over the middle one, and so on.

- It is important to keep an angle of 90° between the bundles. This gives the best plaiting result.

- Often the straws will still be stiff even though they have been soaked. Press the straws together between your thumb and forefinger before the bundle is plaited.

- If the straw becomes very dry during the plaiting lay the plait back into the water for five to ten minutes. Tie the loose end of the plait to prevent it coming apart.

Figure 44-1.

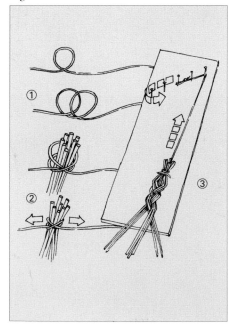

Figure 44-2.

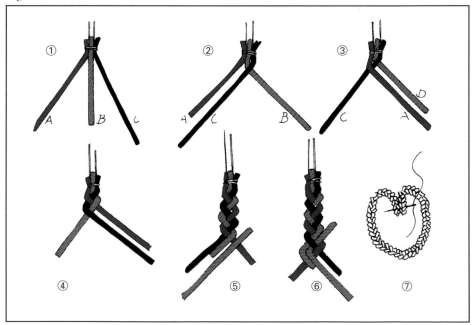

Adding fresh straws during plaiting

• One of the bundles can come to an end before the plait is finished. Stages ⑤ and ⑥ in Figure 44-2 show how to proceed.

⑤ Lay one or more straws on the remains of the bundle.

⑥ Then fold one of the other bundles over it and so on.

• Obviously you will have a problem if all the bundles come to an end at the same time. To avoid this make sure at the beginning that the bundles are of different lengths. Once the plait is finished cut off all bits of straw that stick out.

Finishing

• Tie up the three bundles together once the desired length of plaiting has been achieved. Cut off the remainder of the straws, smooth the wet plait into the required form and sew it up with needle and thread (Figure 44-2 ⑦).

• The plait will require about twenty-four hours to dry completely. While it is drying lay something heavy on it (such as a board) to keep it nice and flat. After drying, trim the ends.

• For decorating and making up plaits see page 56f.

A double straw heart

❖ Waste straw
A red ribbon
Length: inside heart c. 52 cm (20½"); outside heart c. 70 cm (27½")

The double straw heart is a variation of the single heart. The method is the same, only the finishing off is different because the hearts are fixed together.

• Make two plaits of different lengths.

① Fold the longer plait over in the middle and sew up the fold with a few stitches.

② Fold the shorter one over in the middle round the first plait and sew it a bit lower down on to the first plait.

③ Now bend the outside (shortest) plait-ends down to make a heart shape and sew the ends together with a few stitches.

④ Then bend the long inside plait-end round it and sew the ends on to the other heart firmly.

⑤ After drying cut off the inside end of the joined hearts and trim the bottom joint neatly. Hang the hearts up with a red ribbon or red wool.

Figure 45-2.

Figures 45-3.

∨ Figure 45-4.

Figure 45-1.

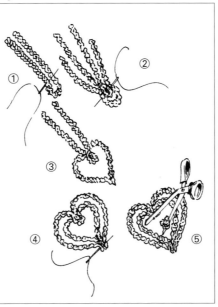

Plaiting a straw wreath

❖ *Wheat or rye straw*
  Length: 70–80 cm (28–32")

With the straw heart the ends were sewn together so that the plaiting was side-on. With a wreath (Figure 46-2) you see the plaiting head-on and the two ends are laid one over the other. Here a tied-up bundle of straws would not look good at the beginning, so

Figure 46-1.

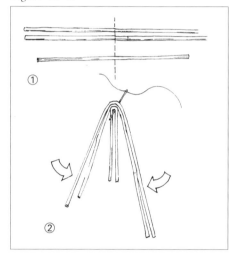

Figure 46-2.

this plaiting is begun in a different way (Figure 46-1).

• Take a bunch of wet straws (some of which are head to tail to make it even) which is only *half* as thick as necessary. Separate into three bundles, making sure they are of different lengths.

• Bend them double (Figure 46-1 ②). Make sure the bundles have different lengths, so that when they are plaited they don't all come to an end together.

• For the rest the plaiting is the same as that of the straw heart (Figure 442). When the plaiting is finished, tie off the ends, and then sew them together tightly.

• Dry this plait *under weight* to prevent the wreath from warping.

Figure 46-3.

Harvest cross with a wreath of ears

❖ *Wheat or rye straws for the plait-work*
  Barley with grains in two rows for the wreath of ears
  Oat and wheat with chaff-husks for the decoration
  Circumference: c. 62 cm (24"); length of the cross: 20 cm (8")

• For plaiting the wreath (Figure 46-3) fifteen straws are needed.

• Plait in the same way as the straw wreath, but add a barley ear (with its two rows of grain) each time on one side during the plaiting. Make sure that the ear sticks out nicely and cannot turn. The barley straw is gripped between the other straws.

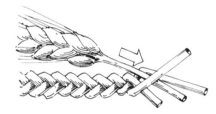

• If the bundle becomes too thick and the plaiting uneven, cut off the barley straws after a few folds. Barley straws are quite thin so that it may be necessary to strengthen them here and there with thin wire.

• Make the cross by sewing one short plait on top of another.

• It is best to sew the cross on to the circle after drying. In the picture the plaiting is decorated with a round oat posy, accentuating the form of the plait-work.

Figure 47-1. >

A "sun" made of ears

❖ *Straws or stalks of the same thickness*
12 wheat-ears with husks
Strong thread

● Cut wetted straws in 12 equal
lengths of 10 cm (4") and flatten them
with an iron.
● Lay six straws one on top of the
other as shown in Figure 48-2. The
first and last straw form a cross enclosing the other straws.
● The thread which binds the crosses
together is passed from behind and
goes over the last straw, under the
next one, and so on. In this way a
twelve-pointed star is produced.
● With the remaining straws make a
second star with twelve points, place
one star on top of the other. Weave a
thread through them, tie them together and cut off the surplus threads.

● Cut every second ray of the star 3
cm (1¼") from the centre, and cut the
remaining long rays into points
(Figure 47-1).
● Take the twelve wheat-ears and cut
off the stalk leaving only a stem of
about 1 cm (½"). Place a bit of glue
on it. Now take the rays, which have
been ironed flat and cut short, between your thumb and forefinger and
one by one press them open and insert the stem of the ear into them.
● Hang this "sun" up in a place where
the husks can also be seen to advantage.

Variation:
In the sun in Figure 48-1 twenty-four
ears are used instead of twelve with alternately a larger and smaller ear.

9 Decorative Straw-Plaiting

A corn-dolly from Wales

❖ *Wheat-straws with ears*
Length: 35 cm (14")

This is a very decorative plait (Figure
49-2) which does need some practice
to make it really beautifully. Practise
with straws which are not so good
(Figure 48-3).

① Tie three wet wheat straws with
ears (*A, B* and *C*) together just below
the ears and fan them out. Now add
two new straws *D* and *E*.
② The new straws are kept in place by
bending straws *A* and *C* round them.
③ The basic technique is shown clear-
ly: straw *B* weaves alternately under
and over (under *E*, over *A*, under *D*
and over *C*). Always begin by going
under, thus finishing by going over the
last straw.

Figure 48-2.

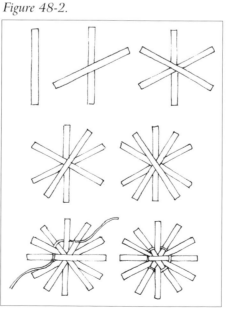

Figure 48-1.

Figure 48-3.

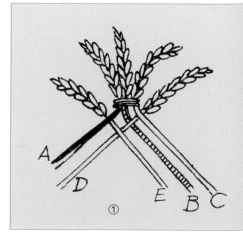

④ ⑤ After every three folds at the edge of the plait add a new straw with the ear protruding. Look carefully at the Figure to see how the new straws are added ensuring an even pattern.

• You can make the plait as long as you like. The corn-dolly in Figure 49-2 consists of twenty-five straws with ears and is 35 cm (14") long.

Figure 49-1.

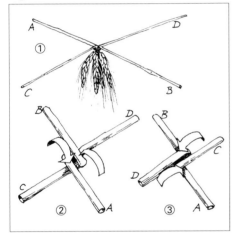

Figure 49-2.

A straw decoration with four-straw plaits

❖ *Eight wheat-straws with ears*
Straws for lengthening
Red ribbon

Four-straw plaiting results in a three-dimensional "rope," rather than a flat braid.

① Tie four wet straws (*A, B, C* and *D*) together just below the ears with strong thread and spread them out at right angles.

Figure 49-3.

② Now fold straw *A* towards *B* and straw *B* to where *A* was.

③ Then fold straw *C* to *D* and straw *DD* to where *C* was.

• Begin again with *A* and *B* and then with *C* and *D*. Continue in this way until the plait is about 18 cm (7") long and then tie the four straws together so that the plaiting does not come apart. Let the unplaited straws just hang for the moment; they should be about 20 cm (8") long.

• Make another plait with four fresh straws. Tie the two plaits together just

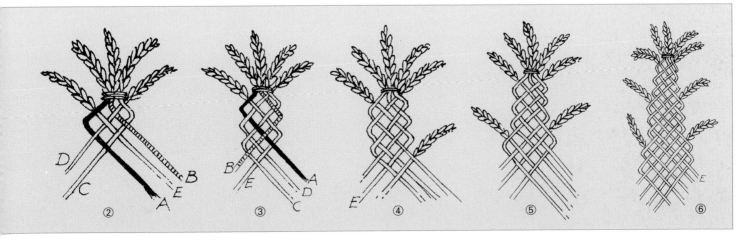

below the ears. Form them into a heart by tying the other ends together, leaving the unplaited straws pointing down (Figure 49-3).

• Tie the unplaited straws with the ears together and cut them off obliquely so they tuck into the base of the heart. Arrange the ears nicely and, if you want to, add a coloured ribbon.

Lengthening the straws:

When plaiting with single straws you cannot add new straws as described earlier (page 45), as it would cause a break in the plaiting.

• Usually the end of the straw is thick. If there is a nodule at the end, cut it off.

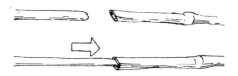

• Take a thinner straw and insert it into the opening of the old straw, gently pushing it as far as it will go. Don't push too hard, or you will split the outside straw.

• Take care when bending over the lengthened straw.

Straw-plaiting with spirals

❖ *Thin long straws*
  Thread

This kind of plaiting which originates in England has various forms with innumerable variations. It is exacting work which must be done with care and patience to ensure even plaiting. Don't be tempted to work too quickly, for the plaiting will become too loose and untidy and this is only noticeable when it is too late to do anything about it.

• Use thin straws which are pliant because they have to be completely folded over. The upper part of the stalks are best. If a stalk has too many nodules, when sharply bent it can break or the nodules protrude and spoil the regular shape of the spiral.

• While plaiting keep a look out for nodules approaching. If necessary cut the straw before the nodule and lengthen it as just described alongside. Take care that the plaiting remains taut while you are extending the straw.

• While you are working you can widen or reduce the plait, or keep the same width.

• Spiral plaiting is always three-dimensional. The technique remains the same whether you make plaiting with three, four or more corners according to the number of straws used.

Spiral plaiting with "padding"

The models in this book have four corners. For this five straws are required. Plaiting with padding is easier because the padding gives support during plaiting. The plaiting forms a kind of long tube and so is less bendable than the plaitings without padding described later.

• Take a bundle of straws, not necessarily all with ears, the minimum number being ten. The thickness of the plait will be affected by the number of straws. For the plaiting on the

Figure 50-1.

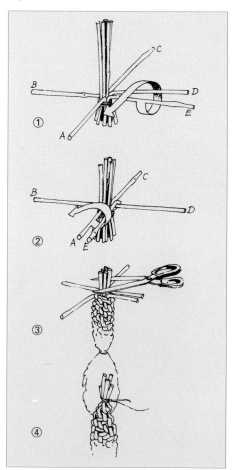

left of Figure 51-1 ten straws with ears are used.

• Tie up the straws together just below the ears (Figure 50-1 ①). Turn the straws upside down so that the ears are pointing down and the stalks up.

① Bend five straws on the outside of the bundle so that they are pointing out horizontally in four directions. The remaining straws form the padding. Work straw *E* under *D* and then back over *D* so that it comes next to straw *A*.
② Then move the plait a quarter-turn anticlockwise so that now straws *A* and *E* are pointing to the right. Now work straw *A* under and over *E* to come next to *B*. Repeat this procedure until the plait has nearly reached the desired length and the straws have become quite short.
③ Now cut the padding off and plait one or two more rows making the plait thinner to finish.
④ Then tie the five straws directly at the top of the plait together.
• Finally cut off the tied straws evenly and if desired adorn the plait with a coloured bow. If the ears make too big a bunch, cut a few off.

Spiral plaiting without "padding"

Once you have learned to plait with padding you can try making hollow spiral plaiting. Take special care that the plait remains taut. The principle has already been described but this kind of plaiting allows the spiral form to become wider or narrower.
• Bringing straw *E* next to *A* (Figure 50-1 ①), but leaving a little gap before laying straw *A* over *E*, allows the plait to become wider as in the spiral on the right of Figure 51-1.
• If *E* lies *on top of A* the plait will retain the same width. If *E* lies to the left of *A* then the plait will become narrower again.

Variation: cup-shaped plaiting
• To make a spiral plait that is open at the bottom finish it off when it has the desired length and is still open instead decreasing it to a point.
• To finishing it off at the last row secure each straw with thread to the straw beside it. Then cut off the bit of straw sticking out.

A mobile of straw spirals

In Figure 51-2 you can see a variety of plaits. Of course you can also use straws with ears.
• The hangers of the mobile are copper wire, and the spirals are hung with red wool to add a bit of colour.

∧ *Figures 51-1.*   *Figure 51-2.* ∨

10 Straw Figures

A straw billy-goat (Yule-buck)

❖ *About 25 straws 45 cm (18") long and*
30 straws 30 cm (12") long
Thin wire (bouquet or florist's wire)
Copper wire
Straw-coloured or other coloured thread

This straw billy-goat (or Yule-Buck)
comes from Sweden (Figure 52-2).
The number and the length of the
straws given are only a guide and can
be varied.

• Wet straw is easily pliant and it can
be dried in its bent form. For the goat
described here the straw has to be
bent quite considerably and so it helps
to use some wire to hold the straw in
shape (Figure 52-1).

• Begin with the *horns*. For these select
two lots of 3 straws which are not too
thick and have a long stretch without
nodules.

① Insert a very thin wire into at least
two of the three straws, tie the three
straws together and make a plait of
about 15 cm (6").

② Roll up the plait and secure it, but
don't cut off the unplaited ends.
Because of the wire plaited with the
straw the horns will remain in the required shape.

• Repeat the above for the second
horn.

• Then take 20 to 25 of the 45 cm
(18") straws for the goat's head, neck
and body. Lay the straws alternately
head to tail so that the thin ends are
evenly distributed. Insert the copper
wire into two straws. If there is a
nodule in the straw push the copper
wire in from both ends up to the
nodule.

③ Now tie the bundle together at one
end (clove-hitch with a few extra
knots, Figure 44-1).

④ Fold it over about 3–4 cm (1½")
from the end. Then insert the horns
into the bundle (the goat's neck) and
secure.

• Now fill the bundle by inserting a
further five to eight straws.

⑤ Fold over the bundle once more to
make the body and this can now be
secured. The wire will hold the bundle
of straws in the required shape.

Figure 52-2. A straw billy-goat.

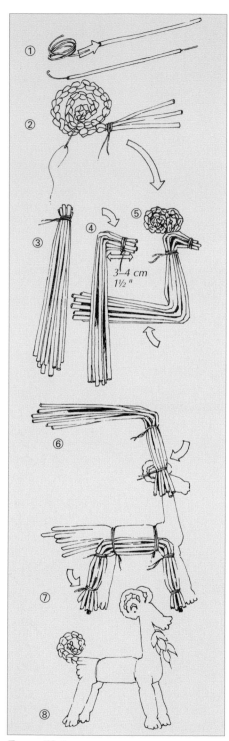

Figure 52-1.

⑥ For the legs take twice 15 straws about 30 cm (12") long. Again insert copper wire into two straws so that the bundle will stand in the right shape. Tie up the forelegs in two places and now make the second bundle similarly.

⑦ Fold the two bundles to make them part of the goat's body and secure behind the forelegs, passing the thread a couple of times round the body before tying. Add a few straws if the body is too thin. Now fold the leg bundles over to make the hindlegs and tie them up in two places.

⑧ From the unfinished end of the head-and-body piece select six straws to plait into a tail after inserting two thin wires into the straws. Then trim the remaining straws. Roll up the plaited tail and trim the legs.

● Bend the horns into a good shape and stick a little bundle of oat-heads or grasses as a tuft below the head in the neck. Now go over all the knots and cut off the loose threads, if necessary putting a touch of glue on the ends.

● For the *head-and-body* piece you need fifteen straws about 35 cm (14") long. The method is roughly the same as that for the straw billy-goat. When tying the head tie in the plaited gills (Figure 53-2 ⑦) and tie in the plaited comb into the neck at the same time.

● For the *legs* we need about twelve straws about 22 cm (9"). Try to select straws without nodules. Insert thin wire into three straws and lay these apart. Insert the thicker copper wire into two other straws.

Figure 53-1. Straw cockerel.

A straw cockerel

❖ *Straws*
Oat-straws or dried grasses
Thin wire
Copper wire
Thread of various colours

① Using damp straw make two plaits, each with three straws. The plait should be about 6–7 cm (2½") long, with loose straw at both ends extending another 3 cm (1¼").
② Tie each plait into a loop. They make the gills of the cockerel.

● For the cockerel's *comb* make three plaits of equal length, but plait only the middle of the straws, leaving about 20 cm (8") at each end of the plait. Tie these plaits into loops.

Figure 53-2.

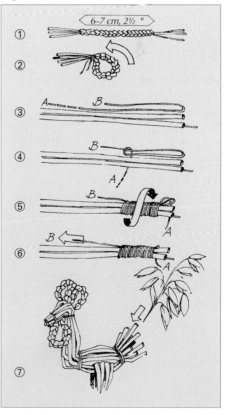

The toes

- Make the toes at the ends of the straws. Because they tend to split when bent over, exposing the wire inside, the ends are finished off with a whipping, which is done as follows.
③ Place one of the straws (which were laid apart) with wire in it and one plain straw together. Lay a loop of the thread over the end of the straw.
④ Pass the long end of the thread round the loop and round both straws.
⑤ Now wind the thread tightly round the loop and both straws until the binding is about 8–10 mm (³⁄₈") wide. Push the end A through the loop and pull the thread tight.
⑥ By pulling B the loop will disappear below the binding. Cut off the visible end A, pull it right under the binding and cut off the end B.
- Repeat this whipping at the other end of the two straws, and then make two more bundles of two straws tied at each end. You now have three lengths of double straw (one plain and one with wire) with each end whipped.
- Put these six straws and the remaining six together into a bundle of twelve and tie the bundle at each end about 5 mm (¼") from the whippings.
- Bend the bundle round to make a U, insert it into the body of the cockerel and tie it in.

The tail

- Now bend the tail up from the body. The wire in the straws will ensure that the straws maintain their shape. Because the rest will dry into shape tie up the tail into one bundle and allow the cockerel to dry.
- When the cockerel is dry cut the tie, and the straws of the tail should fan out. They may need smoothing down here and there.

⑦ Cut the tail straws one by one to different lengths. For the tail wild oats were used which grow at the edge of the fields and have no seeds (the seeds would make the tail too heavy). Alternatively use various grasses.

- Apply a little glue to the ends of the oat-straws or grasses inserted into the tail. Continue with this until you have an ample tail.

- Now bend the whipped toes into the right shape (two toes to the front, and one to the back) and cut off the surplus straw at the "ankle." If you leave the thick copper wire in place you can make the cockerel stand by inserting the wire into two holes in a piece of bark or wood.
- To finish off you can of course use a spray with some water-colour to give the oats or grasses some colour.

Dolls of plaited straw

❖ *9–12 long straws*
  Thread of various colours

- Depending on the thickness of the straws take nine to twelve straws for the plait. Tie the straws together 10 cm (4") from the end (Figure 54-1).
① Plait the long end of the straws to a length of about 12 cm (4½"). Tie up the plait and fold double.
② About 2 cm (¾"–1") from the fold tie both parts of the plait together with button-thread to make the neck. The button-thread is strong enough to make the neck narrower than the head.

- Now plait the arms. In Figure 55-1 there are two methods of plaiting: the women have arms of the usual plait and the men have four-straw plaited arms (see Figure 49-1). With the women's arms you can see the difference between thick and thin straws.
- Make the arms 10 cm (4") long and tie them up well at both sides. Place the arms between the two ends of the large plait directly below the "neck."
③ Now tie up the waist with button-thread at the place where the two ends of the plait are tied together.
④ The lower body of the woman consists of unplaited straws about 7 cm (3") long. In its present form it is still too thin, so lay some bits of straw — preferably without nodules — round

Figure 55-1. >

Figure 54-1.

the waist, hold them tight with one hand and tie these straws with the other hand firmly to the waist.

⑤ Now fold down the straws which are sticking up at the waist. Because these straws which form the skirt tend not to stay in place tie them together loosely from under the skirt.

• Lay the doll in water for some minutes. Allow the doll to dry and then release the tie; the straws should then nearly always stay down.

• In Figure 55-1 one of the women has an "apron" because the straws which were pointing up have been folded down, cut off shorter and tied down with a coloured thread.

• For the man, divide the unplaited straws of the lower body in two after tying up the waist, plait the two halves into legs and tie them at the ends.

• While it is easy to get the women to stand; with the men it is more difficult. It should be possible if the feet are trimmed properly. You can plait a bit of copper wire into the two legs, leaving the wire to protrude a bit and insert it into a bit of bark on which the figure stands.

• For the baby (held by the central doll of Figure 55-1) use some left-over straws, fold them into two and tie them up. Of course the body can also be plaited and you can clothe the dolls with little bits of cloth or dried leaves.

• The basket is made of a plait of three ears. The plaits are sewn together with thread to make a basket. Of course bigger baskets and boxes can be made in the same way by using more straws.

11 Decorating and Assembling

In this chapter there are a few general tips on decorating and setting up, for example, a wreath, a pine-cone or one of the plaits described in the next chapter. These require quite simple techniques using all kinds of things which are to be found in the garden, park, grass-verges or woods. For example:

Cereals and grasses
The leaf-sheaths of the maize-cob
The silks of the corn cob
The tassels (panicles) of corn (maize)
Pine-cones (even the remains gnawed
　by squirrels)
Larch-cones
Alder-cones
Conifer-cones
Acorns
Beech-nuts
Hop-cones
Hogweed-blossom
Honesty-pennies
Dried leaves
Hydrangea flowers
Maple seeds

All these materials must of course be thoroughly dried.

Mounting harvest materials on wire

❖ *Various harvest findings*
　Thin wire (0.4 mm, ¹/₈"–³/₁₆")
　Wire-clippers

To make a bouquet or posy use fine wire to bind together each separate item. Like this grasses, beech-nuts, and so on, can be firmly secured to make an artistic whole. Keep the stems as short as possible, to avoid the posy becoming too thick (Figure 57-1). The wire holds the stems together.

Fixing wire to a stalk
① Take a piece of wire about 15 cm (6") long, bend it double making a loop with one end pointing down.
② Take a straw and hold it tight between your thumb and forefinger so that the loop can be passed round it.
③ Let one end of the wire lie against the stalk and wind the other end three or four times tightly round them. Let

Figure 57-1.

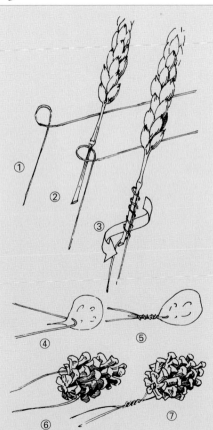

the ends of the wire lie next to each other.
● It is possible to set several stalks together on to wire in this way. Make sure that the two loose ends of the wire are of about the same length, so that when the posy is finished they will give it enough support.

Fixing wire to leaves or honesty-pennies
● Take a fine wire about 15 cm (6") long.
④ Push one end of the wire through the leaf a little bit above the lower edge and bend it carefully downwards.
⑤ Take the leaf between your thumb and forefinger and wind one end of the wire two or three times tightly round the other end and then bring it straight down.

Fixing wire to pine-cones and such like
⑥ Push a wire to be passed through the bottom row of scales near the stalk of a dry cone.
⑦ Twist one end of the wire a few times round the other.

Figure 57-2.

Making a posy

❖ *Various harvest findings*
Thin wire (0.4 mm, $^1/_8$"–$^3/_{16}$")
Wire-clippers

Figure 59-1 shows the various stages in making a posy.
① First choose the materials which you wish to use for the posy and set them on wire (Figure 57-1).
② Begin with a long object such as an ear of corn. Then choose something to go with it. Hold both articles in one hand while with the other twist their wires once round each other — enough to secure them firmly without causing an unnecessary thickening the posy.
③ Now take a leaf or a sprig of conifer, for example, and lay it over the wire of the first two materials. Twist the wire round this once, so that the wire does nor show at the top.

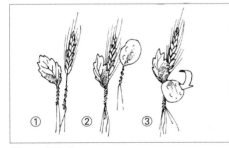

Figure 59-1.

• In this way one thing after the other can be added. Look carefully at the posy from the front so as to see where the next piece is to come, attach it firmly there and don't pull things which are already attached round to one side, for then the whole posy may come adrift.
• To conceal the wire-stems attach one or more leaves to the posy and then bend them back over the wire. You

<   *Figure 58-1.*

may find an opening in the "heart" of the posy which can be filled with something round such as a pine-cone, or a sprig of conifer.
• Once the posy is finished you can take a piece of wire out of the middle and twist this firmly round the other wires, cutting off the end at the required length with your wire-clippers.
• Tie up the posy firmly with a piece of wire — or with needle and thread — round a plaited wreath, a little piece of wood (Figure 57-2) or something similar.

Figure 59-2.

Decorating a pine-cone

❖ *A large pine-cone*
A lump of modelling clay, diameter about 2.5 cm (1")
A piece of thin plastic (as from a plastic bag)
A piece of ribbon
A piece of wire (thickness approx. 0.7 mm, $^1/_{32}$")
Various autumn materials set on wire

For decorating a pine-cone use fitting materials from a wood. When finished it can be hung up or laid down.
• Pass a piece of wire round through the scales near the stem (Figure 57-1 ⑥ and ⑦).
• Place the lump of clay in a little piece of plastic bag (which helps to keep it firm) and with the wire attach it firmly to the pine-cone together with a bow of ribbon. The lump of clay will come to sit more or less between the scales.
• Cut off the wire ends as short as possible, even bending back the sharp ends and sticking them into the lump of clay.
• The pine-cone can now be hung up, and the decorations (already set on wire) can be added.
• The wire should not be too long, as they stick into the lump of clay.
• If it is difficult to insert the materials prick some holes in the plastic with a large needle.

12 Corn-Husk Dolls

Corn (maize) husks were used by Native Americans to make baskets, rugs and playthings. The colonists of the New World learned their skills and passed these back to Europe, where particularly the Czechs are known for their meticulously crafted dolls.

The husks of the corn-cob make up the basic material for these dolls. If you cannot buy corn-cobs with covering leaves, find a farmer who grows maize and ask him for a few cobs.

Preparing the husks

● The husks are brittle, so the cobs must be "peeled" carefully. Cut the husks round the stalk (Figure 60-1). Remove the fuzzy silks carefully from the top of the cob, and dry them well in the sun (if they are not quite dry they can go mouldy). They will come in handy to use as hair.
● The fine, thin husks of the cob are best dried and flattened in a flower-press or a telephone book with a weight on it (if they are dried in the

Figure 60-1.

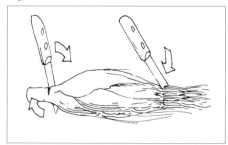

sun they will curl). If the leaves have a yellowish green colour after being dried, lay them out in the sun and the greenish colour will be bleached away.
● Dry the rough, brittle husks of the plant itself in the sun to use as stuffing.
● The dried husks look and can be cut like paper. It is fun to work with, so try to lay in a good store during the harvest.

Making the doll

❖ *Husks of the corn-cob*
  Dried corn silks
  Balls of cotton-wool, cork or polystyrene with a diameter of 8–24 mm (³/₈"–1")
  Cotton wool
  Very thin wire
  Copper wire 0.8 mm (¹/₃₂")
  Button-hole thread in various suitable colours
  Glue
  A large needle or awl
  Pair of scissors

Although the husks are first dried they can generally only be worked when they are moistened to make them pliant. Dry husks have the tendency to break.
● Lay only a few husks in a basin of lukewarm water for five minutes. Note that wet husks expand and shrink again when they are drying.

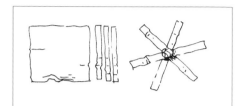

Figure 60-2.

The head
● Begin with the head. You need a little ball as padding which can be of cotton-wool, cork or polystyrene, or even a round wooden bead.

① If none of these is available cut up a dry husk into strips about 5 mm (¼") as in Figure 60-1. Cut along the width (across the veins).
② Make a little ball out of these strips. Stick the ends of the strips together with a bit of glue. The biggest dolls shown here have a head with a diameter of about 25 mm (1").

① With a strong needle or an awl make a hole through the ball and push a piece of wire right through (Figure 61-1).
② Twist the ends together. The wire must not be too short as it will be needed to strengthen the body.
③ Select a good thin (but not too wide) wet husk. Put the ball in the middle and wrap one side of the leaf over the ball. Make sure that the wire passes from the one ear past the chin to the other ear.
④ Now wrap the leaf round the ball with as few folds as possible, keeping the folds to one side of the ball — the back of the head. With buttonhole-thread wrap the leaf as tightly as possible round the neck and secure. To

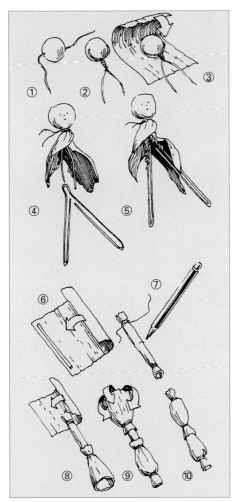

Figure 61-1.

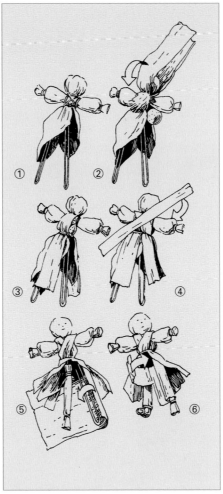

Figure 61-2.

long sleeves. For this use a maize-leaf 6 × 6 cm (2½" × 2½"). The sleeves are puckered and tied inside out to the arms
⑨ Then turned them outside in.
⑩ Secured the sleeves in the middle of the arms. If the sleeves don't puff out, fill them with some left-over husks.

The upper body
① (Figure 61-2) Secure the arms to the head, making sure that a bit of the neck still shows. Choose the side of the head with the least folds to make into the face. Fix the arms to the back of the neck by criss-crossing some thread round them and securing.
② Now fill the body and the back. For this tie two narrow husks (about 3 cm, 1¼" wide) to the middle of the neck immediately above the arms. Fill the back where the arms are secured with a little ball of cotton-wool.
● For the stomach take half a ball of cotton-wool or cork of the same size as the head.
③ Fold the strips of tied-on maize-leaf over the cotton-wool and the half-ball and tie them at the waist with thread.
④ To finish off the shoulders cut a few husk strips about 10–15 mm (½") wide. Lay one of the strips obliquely from the left shoulder to the right side of the waist and secure there. Repeat for the other side. Repeat this again if the side of the upper body is not quite covered.
● Finally do this once more, fastening the strips more loosely round the upper body, so that when they dry and shrink they don't fit too tightly round the body. These last strips form the blouse.

make a neck wind the thread four or five times round the neck and secure again. The rest of the maize-leaf is left to hang. Take a copper wire about 30 cm (12") long. Fold it as shown to make the body and legs.
⑤ Wind the thin wire from the head around the copper leg wires.

The arms
⑥ For the doll's arms take a piece of copper wire (or thin wires twisted together) about 10 cm (4") long.

● Wrap a piece of maize-leaf round the wire. The leaf should stick out about 1 cm (½") at each end and should be about 7–8 cm (3") long depending on the thickness of the leaf (a thin leaf needs to be wrapped more times round otherwise the arms look too thin).
⑦ Tie up the rolled-up leaf just beyond each end of the wire.
Mark the middle of the arms with a pen.
⑧ Give the arms sleeves; the women a half or three-quarter sleeve, the men

61

The lower body (man)

⑤ Make legs and trousers. For this the two ends of the wire are wrapped separately with husks and tied at top and bottom. Then bend the ends of the legs to make a foot. Now make the trousers by wrapping husks round the legs until they are thick enough.

⑥ The last husk is cut and the top wound round the upper body. If necessary stick husk with glue when it is dry.

● To make more baggy trousers, wrap a puckered husk loosely round the leg and secure it only at the thigh.

● Make knickerbockers in the same way as puff-sleeves, but first secure the husk at the "ankle," turn it inside out and secure it at the thighs.

● You can cover all rough ends and loose bits by giving the doll a smock (Figure 62-1).

The lower body (woman)

The lower body of the women can be filled, or simply consist of a skirt and petticoat (Figure 62-2).

① For a filled lower body you can take left-over husks. Cut them into strips, wet them and lay the out as a fan and place the doll on its back in the middle of it.

② Now secure the strips to the waist. Repeat this with the doll lying on its front.

③ Fold the husks above the waist down, and tie them together.

Figure 62-2. Lower body of woman.

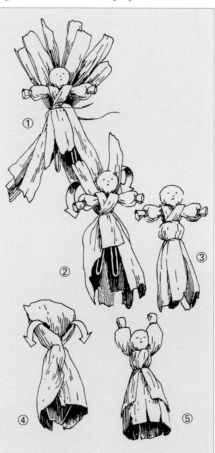

④ Select one or two good (damp) husks and wrap the whole doll up in them, securing them at the waist, bending the arms up beside the head.

● Fold the top half of the husk down and smooth it.

⑤ Trim the bottom of the skirt so that the doll can stand. With this filled skirt it is important that the husks inside are really dry to avoid their going mouldy. To dry the doll put it near a radiator for a few days.

● If you are making a doll with a lower body that is not filled, and which has only a skirt and petticoat then just follow the instructions for the last maize-leaves. Take care that the skirt flounces out well and is firm so that the doll will stand.

● The advantage of this skirt is that you can bend the doll's legs and she can sit or kneel. Make sure that the wire is not visible.

Figure 62-1.

Figure 62-3.

Finishing off
- Once the dolls have been thoroughly dried trim all the edges of the maize-leaves and secure all the loose thread with glue.
- The dolls can now be dressed with dry husks which can be cut and can be stuck on.
- Use the curly silks for hair. They can be plaited if moistened.

- Husks can be coloured by fabric dying or batik. However, it is very laborious for the husks used, and we shall not describe it further here.
- The light tints of the skirts of the dolls shown in Figures 62-1 and 62-3 were obtained by laying the husks in a basin of fairly concentrated water-colours for half an hour, and then rinsing them in clean water. Dry the husks afterwards in a flower-press.
- You can colour the husks with a spray before cutting out the clothing. Alternatively colour the finished doll with a paintbrush and water-colours.

13 Harvest Materials from Woods and Fields

Figure 58-1 shows some of the things which can be found in autumn. Mostly they can be picked from the ground, without harming any trees or plants.

For instance, chestnuts, Spanish chestnuts, acorns, beech-nuts, pine-cones, fir-cones, corn on the cob and corn silks, hazelnuts, rosehips, little feathers, maple seeds, lime-tree seeds, honesty pennies, and so on, can provide hours of imaginative play for young children.

Keep the collection of materials in a dry place with plenty of air. Take care especially with chestnuts and acorns that they don't go mouldy (so don't keep them in a plastic bag). You can store different kinds of cereals, grasses and tassels in tall glasses. For other materials simple cardboard trays are handy.

Dolls and animals from chestnuts, acorns and other materials

❖ *Spanish and ordinary chestnuts*
 Acorns
 Grains of corn (maize), corn husks and silks
 Hazelnuts
 Beech-nut husks
 Rosehips
 Cocktail sticks or wooden barbecue-skewers
 Copper wire
 A straw
 Sunflower seeds
 Sycamore or maple seeds

- Select a few good chestnuts of the right proportions for the head and body parts of the person.
- With an awl or bodkin (or even a darning needle) make holes in the chestnuts and join them together with a piece of a cocktail stick.

A cardboard storage tray

❖ *Stout paper or thin card (8½" × 11", A4, or larger)*

① Fold the paper or card in half and half again, once along the long side and once on the short side.
② Raise the long sides first, then raise one of the short sides, fold the corner inwards and glue it together.
③ Fold the overlapping piece to the short side inwards and stick it with a bit of glue. Do the same with the other short side and the tray is finished.

Figure 63-1.

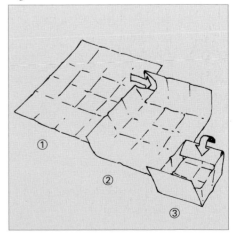

• Insert a piece of copper wire for the arms at the right height in the upper body (first boring a hole if necessary). The upper part of the arms can be made of acorns which should be bored beforehand; the lower part of the arms are made of maize-grains, threaded on to the copper wire, and the hands are made of little bits of straw. The wire enables you to bend the arms.
• Make the legs from cocktail sticks inserted firmly into holes bored in the chestnut. Cut an acorn lengthwise through the middle to make a pair of shoes.
• The woman in Figure 65-1 is finished off with an apron made from a corn husk and some hair made from the silks.
• The man has an acorn hat and smokes an acorn pipe.
• The dog is made of two acorns, a pair of sunflower seeds for his ears (cut slits in the head for the ears) and cocktail sticks.

• The materials used for the dolls in Figure 65-2 are self-evident. The basket on the woman's arm is made of half a walnut and the handle from a strip of corn husk.
• The sprig of honesty-pennies in the background stands in a disc cut from a branch.

• For the dolls in Figure 65-4 acorn-cups, a shell from a chestnut and rose-hips as well as other things are used.

• In Figure 65-5 flat chestnuts or half acorns are used for the birds to prevent them from falling over. To make the wings use sycamore or maple seed wings.

A snake made of acorns

❖ *Acorns*
A rosehip
A red autumn leaf
Copper wire

• Bore a little hole lengthwise in the acorn and thread the acorn on to the copper wire. Do not make the holes too big — the acorns should sit tightly on the wire.
• For the eyes use two tiny pieces of rosehip peel, glue them on to sockets previously made in the head.
• Finally insert into the little cut-open mouth a good firm red autumn leaf (Figure 65-7).

A pine-cone owl

❖ *A pine-cone*
Pine-needles
Two acorn-cups with stems
A beech-nut
Sycamore or maple seed wings

① With a piece of sandpaper flatten the bottom of the pine-cone (Figure 64-1), so that the owl will not fall over.
② Take single sycamore or maple seed wings, cut off the thick seed leaving only the wings. Stick three wings together to make each foot for the owl. When the feet are dry, glue them to the bottom of the pine-cone.
• With an awl, bodkin or thick needle make a hole in the beech-nut and thread a piece of fine wire (florist's wire) through it to secure the beech-nut (the owl's beak) between the scales of the pine-cone.

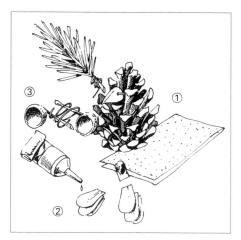

Figure 64-1. Pine-cone owl.

③ Bind the stalks of the acorn-cups together with fine wire and then using the same wire secure the two cups between the scales of the pine-cone so that the beak fits nicely between the two acorn-cup eyes.
• If necessary remove some of the scales to get the eyes into their proper place.
• Finally take a pine twig and secure it to the top of the pine-cone with fine wire (Figure 65-3).

Pine-cone mice

❖ *Pointed pine-cones*
Dried lime-tree seeds
Corn silks or strips of moss

• The mice shown in Figure 65-3 are very simple to make. Select very pointed pine-cones with the scales still closed.
• Make a little hole in the bottom where the stalk joins and glue in the tail which can be made from various materials, for instance wet silks twisted into a thin streamer, strands of

Figure 65-1.

Figure 65-2.

Figure 65-3. Pine-cone owl and mice.

Figure 65-4.

Figure 65-7. Acorn snake

Figure 65-5. Chestnut birds.

Figure 65-6. Pine-cone birds.

Figure 65-8.

moss or simply a thin strip of leather or a piece of wool.

● The glued-on eyes can be made from a tiny twig, as with the smallest mouse; or as with the other mice, from half a lime seed. On the tree these seeds have a grey-green colour, but when dry they harden and turn almost black.

Winged creatures

❖ *Pine-cones*
  Larch-cones
  Acorns with cups
  Feathers
  Beech-nuts
  Maple seeds
  Lime-tree seeds with wings
  Small downy feathers

● The birds in Figure 65-6 have pine-cone or fir-cone bodies. For the heads various materials are used; an acorn with cup and stalk, a little pine-cone or larch-cone with stalk. Fasten them to the body by their stalks or with a twig and glue them on, boring a hole first if necessary.
● For the wings and tail various materials are used: the wings of lime-tree seeds, the wings of maple or sycamore seeds and little downy feathers. The hanging birds of Figure 65-8 have real down feathers.

Variation:
● Make a number of *flying* birds and assemble them to make a *bird-mobile*, as with the plaited spirals in Figure 51-2 or attach them to a hoop as with the bee-mobile in Figure 66-2.

A pine-cone decoration

❖ *A pine-cone*
  All sorts of grasses, plant tassels (panicles), and so on

● Select a nice round pine-cone and stick on all kinds of grasses and tassels (panicles) between the scales in a circle round it.
● It is best not to try to stick everything on at once, but to work layer by layer, looking all the while to see where something can be added in order to keep a harmonious appearance.
● First stick on a number of well-spaced grasses and allow them to dry before proceeding. This drying is best done by placing the pine cone in an egg-cup allowing the stalks of the grasses to rest on the rim.● Once the first ring has dried you can start putting in and gluing the next.

Figure 66-1.

A bee-mobile

❖ *Alder-cones*
  Maple seeds
  A piece of rattan (cane)

● Cut off the seed-globules from the maple seed wings and glue the wings into the alder cones. Tie a thin thread round the middle of the bees so that they can fly.
● Make a hoop from a bit of rattan. If the rattan is too pliant take two canes gluing or tying the two ends together.
● Now hang the bees up at different heights on to the hoop (Figure 66-2).

Figure 66-2.

Figure 67-1. Teasel spider and hedgehog.

A teasel-head spider

❖ *A teasel*

• A scary spider can be made from the long lower prickles of a teasel.
• First cut off the stalk completely, then cut out the spider and hang it up on a thread (Figs 67-1).

A teasel hedgehog

❖ *A teasel*
 Lime-tree seed-cups

You may be lucky and see a hedgehog with young ones following in a line behind: father hedgehog, mother hedgehog and then the baby hedge-hogs.
• Cut off some of the stalk of the teasel but leave about 5 mm (¼") for its nose.
• Cut away the long spidery bits round the snout and make one side flat by cutting away the prickles with a pair of scissors.
• Cut a few dried black lime-tree seeds through the middle: one half is for the snout, two other halves are stuck on for the eyes.

Figure 67-3. A pine-cone troll.

Pine-cone trolls

❖ *Hazelnut cups*
 Pine-cones and fir-cones
 Corn (maize) silks
 Alder-cones
 Fine wire

• For the bodies of the two trolls in Figure 67-4 a pine-cone and a fir-cone are used.
• Cut off the tops of the pine-cones to make a flat top.

Figure 67-2. Teasel hedgehog family.

Figure 67-4. Pine-cone trolls.

- Turn the cones upside-down and the flat top now becomes a base and the cones will stand. If necessary secure what is now the bottom row with a bit of beeswax or a bit of clay.
- Select a few suitable hazelnut cups and look carefully to see which side looks most like a face.
- Tie a piece of fine wire between the wild "hairs" of the nut cups so as to be able to tie the head on to the body of a pine-cone.
- Tie the head on to the pine-cone body with fine wire between the scales so that it cannot be seen (Figure 67-3).
- For the arms you can use alder-cones, inserting them with their twigs between the scales of the pine-cone and gluing them in.
- If there is any wire left over after attaching the head to the body use it for the arms by winding some maize-hair round the wire.
- For the feet you can use pine-scales gluing them on or tying them with fine wire, threading them on to the wire first before attaching them to the body. You can also fill up the hollow space at the feet with some clay to get the troll to stand better.
- The feet of the smallest troll were made from a piece of pine-cone which had been nibbled away by squirrels.

< Figure 68-1.

Autumn garlands

Autumn garlands can be made using all sorts of materials. While you are out walking in the country have a good look round to see what can be found in the way of ripe fruits and seeds.

Suitable materials are: fresh grains of corn (maize) and silks, dried leaves, rosehips, beech-nuts and their husks, acorns and acorn-cups, chestnuts, hazelnuts, straws, Spanish chestnut conker-husks, pumpkin seeds, hop-cones and so on.

Mobile with autumn garlands

All the fruits, chestnuts, nuts etc. on the garlands hanging down from this mobile are separated by little bits of straw of different lengths. To cut these straws, make a quick snip with a pair of very sharp scissors. If you cut too slowly, the scissors will flatten the straw and it may break.

As can be seen in Figure 69-1 many different things have been used for the garland, even little twig and corn silks.

In this example a ring of plaited straw is used for the mobile other materials and forms are of course possible.

Garlands for windows

Depending on what materials you have collected you can adorn your window. For example thread some dried leaves carefully on to a strong thread, making sure that they are well spaced, so that the shapes can readily be seen. Of course you can also take leaves which are not yet dry, but they have the disadvantage of curling up and losing their colour in a heated room. If the leaves are well dried they will generally keep their colours (see page 70 for how to dry leaves).

Figure 69-1.

14 Harvest Leaves

Make a loop in the thread at both ends of the garland and fix it in place with pins on to the window-frame or tape it to the window itself.
• If you are using corn grains take the fresh soft ones straight from the cob. If these are not available it is possible to take dried grains and boil them till they become soft.
• Before threading bore a little hole in the beech-nut husks. Do the same for the acorns, acorn-cups and hazelnuts which have already been dried. If the pumpkin-seeds are still fresh and moist the needle will easily go right through them. But with dried seeds you must first bore a hole.
• Of course it is not necessary to hang up all the garlands at the same time as is shown on Figure 68-1. Some of the fruits will slowly but surely shrivel up. So after a time an old garland can be replaced by a fresh one.

• You can sometimes make a more attractive garland by not threading the fruits and nuts right up against each other and then thread lengths of straw in between.

Many things can be made with dried leaves. It can become an absorbing activity to look for brightly-coloured autumn leaves. Medium-sized and smaller ones are most suitable. Collect leaves of many different shapes, for when arranging a pattern variety enhances the design.
• Store dried leaves according to their kind, colour or size, in large envelopes.
• The leaves must however be thoroughly dry beforehand to prevent their becoming mouldy.

Working with fresh leaves

❖ *Fresh autumn leaves*
   Wallpaper or flour paste

With autumn leaves you can of course make all sorts of things. Little children will nearly always want to do something right away with all the leaves which they have been collecting.
• Something which they can do is to stick the leaves on to the outside of a window with some paste. After a time the leaves will dry, many shrivel up and lose their colour, so with a little warm water all the bits can be washed off the window.

Drying leaves

• The simplest way of drying autumn leaves is to lay them in an old telephone book, and leave them for about a week. Put some heavy books or bricks on top of the telephone book, to press the leaves flat.
• A flower-press or leaf-press is also useful (see p.41).
• Not all leaves lend themselves to being dried, for there are leaves, such as birch for example, which in the process of being dried lose their colour completely and become quite brown. Other leaves, such as chestnut are best picked off the tree while the inside of the leaf is still green and a little yellow-brownish edge appears round it.

A window decoration of dried leaves

❖ *Autumn leaves*
   A large sheet of tracing paper
   Modelling cement or glue

Figure 71-1 shows an ornamental border of dried autumn leaves.
• Don't glue or cement the leaves directly on to the window because scraping them off again entails a lot of work (though paste can be washed off with warm water). It is also easier to make the border lying flat to try out the colour-layering and leaf combinations.

Figure. 71-1. >

• Take a large sheet of tracing paper, cut to the size of the window. Cut out the centre of the tracing paper (the border-frame can also be made with strips of paper joined together). The decoration shown was made on a border frame 10 cm (4") wide.
• Lay out the decorations loose on to the paper so that you can see when the combination is right.
• Make sure the edges of the tracing paper are completely covered with leaves and no longer visible once the decoration is finished

• Begin by arranging on a table a number of leaves overlapping each other to make a corner. Keep rearranging the leaves until they give a pleasing appearance, but take care with them as dried leaves are brittle.
• Then stick the leaves one by one on to the tracing paper in the right place. Because the leaves have been dried it is best not to use a water-based paste. Modelling cement is the best: it sticks well and dries quickly. Remove surplus adhesive quickly.

• After each item allow the glue to dry so that everything remains in place. Lay something heavy on top (such as a thick book).
• If you don't want to wait while the first batch is drying, continue in another corner. While the glue is drying there you can go back to the first part.
• When the border is finished it can be stuck to the inside of a window with some adhesive tape.
• After removing it the decoration can be stored between two sheets of card.

Harvest transparency

❖ *Dried leaves and grasses*
  Stout cardboard
  Tracing paper
  Modelling cement

• Cut out a frame from the cardboard. The form can be rectangular, circular or oval as desired.
• Draw the outline of the frame again on the tracing paper. Select some good

leaves and/or grasses. Stick these with as little glue as possible on to the tracing paper.
• Finally stick the cardboard frame on to it and dry the whole thing under weight.

Postcards and notepaper

❖ *Autumn leaves*
  Card
  Sheets of notepaper
  Plastic foil, sticky on one side

Figure 72-2 shows some cards and notepaper simply decorated with leaves. Often only one beautifully shaped leaf is all that is necessary, but it is also possible to embellish a whole card making your own picture postcard.
• Cement the dried leaves on to the paper or card and allow it to dry under weight.
• With a picture postcard it is better to cover the leaves with plastic foil.

Figure 72-1. Harvest transparency.

Figure 72-2. Postcards and notepaper.

Figure 72-3. A crown of leaves.

A crown of leaves

❖ *Large autumn leaves, for example,*
  sycamore or maple

Figure 72-3 shows how this crown of
leaves is made.
- First cut off the stems and keep
them.
- Lay one leaf partly over another and
press a stem through them both to
keep them together. Continue until
the crown has reached the desired
length.
- If necessary strengthen the crown by
sticking a strip of sticky tape along
the inside. Finally stick the two ends
together and the crown is finished.

15 Autumn, Michaelmas and Hallowe'en

Michael and the dragon from harvest leaves

❖ *Autumn leaves*
  Tracing paper

Making Michael and the dragon from
dried leaves is similar to the window
decoration on page 71-1. This time
not only the border is decorated, but a
whole picture is made.
- Cut the tracing paper to fit the window frame.
- First sketch out on a piece of paper
what you have in mind.
- Then begin at one corner of the
paper to lay the leaves but this time
without overlapping.
- Make sure that when the parts are
finished they are dried under weight.
It is unnecessary to cover the whole
sheet — leave some parts open to
allow light to shine through, as in
Figure 73-1.

Figure 73-1. Michael and the dragon.

Cobwebs

❖ *A fine big chestnut*
  Barbecue-skewers or cocktail-sticks
  Coloured wool
  Silver thread
  An awl or large needle

- With the awl or large needle make
at least seven holes round the chestnut. Then insert a cocktail stick or
barbecue skewer into each hole. For a
large cobweb use barbecue skewers,
for a small cobweb cocktail-sticks.
- Select a coloured wool, tie one end
on to one of the sticks and press the
wool hard against the chestnut. Lead
the wool from stick to stick, and
round each stick. Continue until a
colour strip becomes quite evident.
- Cut the wool, and tie on another
colour and continue.
- Make the knots as small as possible
and see that they lie at the back of

Figure 73-2. A cobweb.

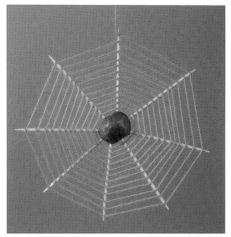

Figures 74-1.

∧ *Figures 74-2.*　　*Figure 74-3.* ∨

the web. The nicer side of the chestnut is of course the front. By changing the colours you get the effect shown in Figure 73-2.

● Finish off by tying the wool on to one of the sticks.

Variation 1:

The cobweb in Figure 74-1 is on the same principle.

● Use only one colour, and leave space between the rounds, so that a real web is made.

Variation 2:

The cobweb in Figure 74-3 uses silver thread, giving the appearance of dew on the cobweb.

● Instead of barbecue skewers use four thin branches to make a frame and drill two or three holes at intervals through each branch.

● Now make a number of holes right through the chestnut.

● Thrust the needle and silver thread first through a hole in one of the twigs and then through the chestnut and then again through a hole in the twig of the frame on the other side (for example from top right to bottom left). Plug the thread temporarily into the frame with broken cocktail sticks or matchsticks.

● When all the threads have been attached to the chestnut, pull out a cocktail sticks and pull the threads tight. Then thrust the stick firmly into the frame and cut off the protruding bit.

● Repeat for each cocktail stick.

● Now start weaving the web. When the cobweb is big enough tie the end with a little knot and cut off the surplus threads.

● Finally you can make two holes to hang up the cobweb frame.

A dragon made of chestnut husks

❖ *Conker husks or horse-chestnut husks*
 Cocktail-sticks
 Chestnut leaves
 Red berries or rosehips

● Select a number of chestnut husks which are still closed. Use a husk which is a little open for the mouth.

● Attach the husks to each other with cocktail-sticks. Figure 74-3 shows what still has to be done to make the dragon look fierce. Let your imagination run freely.

A dragon-loaf

❖ *About 500 g (18 oz) white flour, fine wheatmeal or a mixture of both*
 275 ml (10 fl oz) lukewarm milk
 ½ tablespoon yeast
 50 g (1¾ oz) hard butter
 Just under ½ tablespoon salt
 1 yolk of an egg (optional)

● Measure the flour into a mixing-bowl and make a hole in the middle (keep back a few spoonfuls for kneading). Dissolve the yeast into the milk, pour the mixture into the hole in the flour and stir it from the middle outwards bringing in the flour to make a runny rough.

● Cut the butter into very thin strips and lay these on top of the dough. Sprinkle the salt on to the butter.

● Leave this mixture to stand for a quarter of an hour until bubbles have formed. During fermentation some warmth is released and the butter is softened. Now you can lay the yolk over it. Stir it all with a fork from the middle outwards till it becomes a firm but tacky dough.

• Now sprinkle the remains of the flour on to the kneading board, empty the dough scraping the dish, sprinkle some of the flour over the dough and knead it all to an elastic dough until it no longer sticks to the board or to your hands, using more flour if necessary. Don't knead for too long, otherwise the warmth of your hands will melt the butter and you will press it out and the dough will become sticky.

• Now put the lump of dough back into the bowl. Put the bowl into a plastic bag or cover it with a damp cloth and allow the dough to rise to twice its volume in room temperature (1–2 hours) or in the refrigerator (3 hours or overnight). Dough which has risen cold is more easily formed.

• Now shape the dough into the form of a dragon, lay it on to a baking-tray and allow it once more to rise to twice its volume (loosely covered with cling-film at room temperature). Paint the loaf with egg-yolk loosely stirred with the same amount of milk or water.

Bake 10 minutes at 225°C, (450°F, gasmark 7–8) and then 15 minutes at 200°C (400°F, gasmark 6).

Figure 75-1. Dragon-loaf

A Hallowe'en lantern

❖ *A turnip or pumpkin*
A sharp knife
A spoon
An apple-corer
A night-light in a tin
Wire

• Cut a slab about 2–3 cm (1") thick from the top of the pumpkin or turnip.

• Hollow the turnip out by using a knife, spoon or apple-corer. This is best done by sticking the apple-corer into the turnip each time and then scooping out the loose bits with a spoon. Continue until the turnip is completely hollowed out. The walls of the turnip should remain about 5–10 mm (¼"–½") thick.

• Make the bottom flat with a hole in the middle to take the night-light.

• With a sharp knife carve out carefully sun, moon and stars in the outside of the turnip without cutting through the walls, these designs being peeled off.

• With the apple-corer make three holes in the lid for air to allow the light to burn. Insert the wire left and right through the turnip and through the lid. Make the loops big enough so that the lid can be moved up and down for lighting the light.

Candle decorations
See page 80.

Figure 75-2. Hallowe'en Lantern.

Figure 75-3.

16 Transparencies

❖ *Coloured card (170 gsm)*
Tissue-paper
Tracing paper
Glue
A pair of sharp scissors

Basic forms

• *Transparencies with a cardboard frame.*
These are suitable for hanging in the
window, or for standing on a table.
• *Transparencies without a frame.* The
picture is made with coloured tissue
paper stuck on to the tracing paper.

General instructions

• When making transparencies it is
best to start with a white background.
A glass table with a lamp under it or a
box with a light inside is very useful
when making transparencies.
• When choosing the colours take into
account the mixed colours that will
appear when two layers of differently
coloured tissue-paper are laid one over
the other. Sometimes the result is
quite surprising!
• Draw the outlines on the tissue-
paper with a sharp pencil, because
when you are cutting out the forms
the pencil lines must be cut away too.

• When cutting out the forms use a
pair of small sharp scissors and take
plenty of time because it is not as easy
as it looks.
• When gluing layers together use as
little glue as possible and spread it as
thinly as possible; blobs remain visible. Water-based glue is quite ade-
quate and can be undone if necessary.
However, a disadvantage of this kind
of adhesive is that the sheets become
unstuck after a time. A glue-stick can
also be used.

*Transparencies which are hung on
the window can be subject to conden-
sation even with double glazing. Put
a plastic sheet or saran wrap between the window and the transparency to avoid damage.*

Simple transparency with a frame

These simple transparency can be
hung in front of the window. Spring
or Easter subjects can be depicted, for
example the Easter hare, a chicken or
a cock.

The simplest transparency is shown
in Figure 77-2 where the picture is cut
out of card, and a coloured piece of
tissue paper is stuck to the back.

The more complicated transparency
of the angel in Figure 77-9 is made
from several layers of yellow tissue-
paper.

• Draw the shape of the transparency
as well as the inside design onto the
back of a piece of strong, coloured
card.
• Cut out the outside shape of the
transparency out.
• The cut the picture inside with a
pair of sharp scissors or a sharp knife.
• Stick a sheet of tissue-paper on to
the back of the card frame (the side
on which there are pencil marks).
• Make a loop to hang the transparency with a needle and thread.

Figure 77-1.

Figure 77-2.

Figure 77-3.

Figure 77-4.

Figure 77-5.

Figure 77-6.

∨ Figure 77-7.

∨ Figure 77-8.

∨ Figure 77-9.

Simple "stained glass" transparencies

This technique gives the effect of stained glass panes set in lead (Figure 77-5).

① First draw the design and the frame of the transparency on white tracing paper and then transfer the forms to the (dark blue) drawing-paper by using carbon paper; or you can draw the design straight on to the drawing-paper.

② Cut out the design and the frame-work using sharp scissors or a knife.

③ Lay tissue-paper of the chosen colour on top of the drawing on the white tracing paper. The outlines of the drawing will be visible through the tissue-paper. With a pencil trace the figures or details appropriate to this colour on to the tissue-paper. Make the outlines on the tissue-paper a little bigger than the original outlines on the drawing.

④ Cut out the figure on the coloured tissue-paper and stick this on at the back of the blue drawing-paper all round the opening using as little glue as possible. (You can use a matchstick to smear a tiny bit of glue along the edges of the drawing.)

• In this way stick colour by colour behind the opening. When two colours of tissue-paper are stuck over each other new colours are created.

• Finally stick the transparency on to the window with two tiny strips of double-sided adhesive tape.

"Stained glass" window triptych

Make a simple triptych (Figure 77-6) in the same way as the previous transparency. You can set this on a table or shelf with a night light behind it.

• Once you have cut out the frame, crease it with a blunt knife or dried-up ballpoint pen to make neat folds.

• The three colours of the shepherds are made here with two colours of tissue-paper. The shepherd on the left is made with brown tissue-paper except

Figure 78-1.

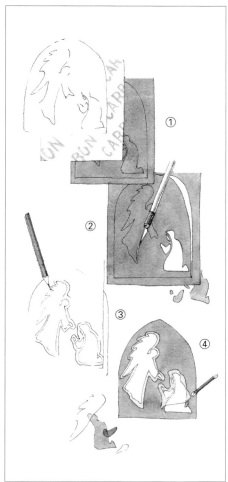

for his boots, and his trousers and arms are also covered with red.

• The shepherd on the right requires green for his cap and purple for his shoes. Instead of one layer of a particular colour you can, of course, use two, as with Joseph's clothes and his staff.

Window triptych

Instead of the stained glass window effect you can cut out a big "window" in the frame which takes out the greatest portion of the front of the triptych.

• Choose the method of making the picture:

1. In Figure 77-4 the boy is cut out as a silhouette, and the coloured tissue paper is added behind.
2. In Figure 77-7 Mary, Joseph and the ass are cut out of card, and then covered with tissue paper.

• Cut the outside shape from card and crease the folds with a blunt knife or dried-out ballpoint pen. Cut out the inside shape.

• Trace the opening on a sheet of tracing paper.• Out of coloured tissue paper tear the shapes you want as background. Stick the pieces of tissue-paper on to the tracing paper and slowly build up the transparency layer by layer.

• Finally cut out tracing paper (with the design) about 1 cm (½") beyond the edge you drew first. Then stick it on to the back of the card frame with the tissue paper to the front.

Transparency without a frame

- Mark the shape of the transparency on to a sheet of tracing paper. Lay it on a light table, or stick in to the window.
- Figure 77-3 has been made by tearing the tissue paper. If you are not confident of making a freehand picture, draw the picture on paper and lay it under the tracing paper.

Figure 79-1.

- Tearing the paper instead of cutting gives a very free effect.
- Using different layers and colours of tissue-paper will give rich colour shadings and depth.
- Only rarely will you need to tear a piece into an exact shape (like the sword), the main part of the picture is built up of random torn-out shape.

A simple window transparency

❖ *Tissue-papers of various colours*
   Tracing paper
   Glue or glue-stick
   A sharp pair of scissors

- The technique described here uses only tissue-paper which allows the colours full scope and provides endless variations.
- The angel in Figure 77-8 is made from two layers of yellow tissue-paper and a layer of white tissue-paper as cover.
- First draw the design on the white tracing paper.
① Then for each layer of tissue-paper draw the requisite detailed copy on a separate sheet of tracing paper. The yellow angel thus consists of the two top figures in Figure 79-1.
- Lay the first sheet of yellow tissue-paper on top of the first drawing and with a sharp pencil trace the figure. Cut it out.
② Lay the cut-out sheet on the second drawing and move it around until the two drawings fit. Then lay the second sheet of yellow tissue-paper exactly over the first, put the second drawing over and cut it out.

- Stick the two sheets together only at the edges at a few points, and do the

same with the white sheet of tissue-paper. Finally, with a tiny bit of glue stick down any loose ends of the angel.

Variation
The blue angel of Figure 77-9 has one layer more than the yellow angel: this transparency consists of two layers of light blue and one layer of pink or mauve tissue-paper. The method is the same.

- When sticking them together make sure that the cut-out figures fit exactly over each other, the outside edge can be trimmed later.

Figure 79-2.

17 Candles

Candles are used mainly in the dark time of year, though they can be used for special occasions throughout the year. When decorating them you can choose a motif for the festival of the season.

Dipped candles

❖ *Beeswax or candle stubs*
Candle wick or a thick cotton yarn
Tall narrow tins
A saucepan of hot water
A hotplate or spirit-stove

Dipping candles requires much patience.

• Put some water in a saucepan to boil. Put the bits of wax or candle-stubs in a tall narrow tin, and put the tin into the saucepan of heating water to melt the wax. The depth of the wax in the tin will determine the maximum length of the candles. When the wax has melted, the saucepan can be transferred to a hotplate or spirit-stove on the table.

• Lay some newspaper underneath to catch any spilt candle-grease. Keep topping up the water to replace what has evaporated.

• Wax takes a long time to melt and as it then slowly solidifies on the hotplate it is a good idea to have a second tin of melted wax ready to hand.

• For the wick cut a length of candle wick or cotton yarn long enough to prevent children getting their fingers into the hot wax. Before dipping pull the wick taut with both hands so that the finished candle will be straight.

• Dip the wick into the hot wax for a moment, draw it out again and allow the wax on it to set before dipping the wick in again. In this way a new layer is added each time.

• At the base of the candle a blob of wax will form and grow bigger each time the candle is dipped. Cut this blob off with a knife from time to time.

• Once the candle is finished leave it to cool and harden. This can take several hours, so it is a good idea to hang the candle up by the wick to prevent it being damaged.

The hot water and the wax are very hot! Young children should only dip candles under adult supervision.

Decorated candles

❖ *A thick candle*
Candle decorating wax in various
  colours
A thick knitting-needle or a spatula

As shown on page 81 candles can be decorated using various techniques. In each case the wax must first be made workable.

• Take small pieces and knead them well until the wax has become warm and soft.

• The simplest method of decorating candles is to stick little bits of coloured wax on to the candle and then work them into shape.

• You can use a spatula or knitting-needle to shape the finer details. New colours can be made by thoroughly kneading two different coloured bits of wax together (as for example red and yellow making orange).

• Make sure that the coloured wax is properly warmed when you press it on to the candle otherwise it will not stick on properly and may come un-stuck later.

Figure 80-1.

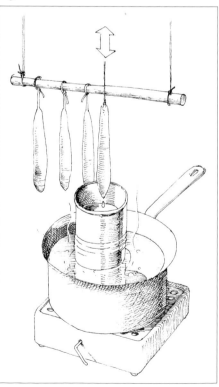

Figure 81-1.

∨ *Figure 81-4.*

Figure 81-2.

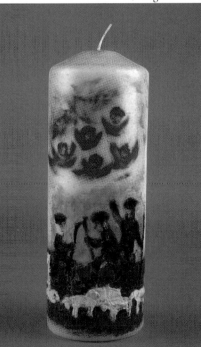

Figure 81-3.

∨ *Figure 81-5.*

∨ *Figure 81-6.*

Decorating candles by smearing

❖ *A thick candle (off-white or white)*
  A piece of fine sandpaper
  Candle decorating wax in various
    colours
  A thick knitting-needle or a spatula

• Use a piece of fine sandpaper to roughen the place on the candle where you wish to place the decoration.
• Warm a small piece of beeswax between your fingers beginning with the lightest colour. Press a little bit of beeswax on to the candle and smear it out very thinly with your warm fingers to give a transparent effect. Now layer the darker colours carefully over the lighter ones.
• Use a knitting-needle or a spatula to define the details; by scratching the wax or by pulling it up you can make forms in relief. Kneading different colours together for a long time will produce new colours.
• The colours black, white, gold and silver are not transparent and so are less used in this method.
• This technique requires some practice, but does give a special effect to the candle.

Figure 82-1.

Clay candlesticks

❖ *Clay*
  A candle
  Water-colours and paintbrush
  Transparent varnish
  Sprigs of green

During Advent, modelling can be a wonderful occupation, and you can make candlesticks with a great variety of shapes: for instance, simply a cube, or an angel carrying a candle between the wings. Put a little saucer underneath to catch the candle-wax and avoid it dripping on to the table or your clothes.
• Make the candlestick out of one piece so that you don't have any bits of clay stuck on. These often come unstuck when the candlestick dries.
• Although you can make the candle-hole to take a particular candle, you must take the candle out of the hole while the clay is still wet because it contracts while drying and so can split if the candle is left in.
• Decorate the candlestick: you can stick sprigs of fir, holly, gold-painted acorns, etc. in the clay while it is still soft, and in this way it becomes a Christmas table decoration. Make sure that the sprigs are not too close to the candle flame.
  Allow the candlestick to dry out thoroughly and then you can paint it with water-colours. Once the water-colours are dry the candlestick can be varnished.
  See also Figure 75-3.

18   Advent

Advent begins on the fourth Sunday before Christmas and lasts till Christmas itself. If Christmas Eve is on a Saturday, the first Sunday in Advent will fall already on November 27, and Advent lasts four full weeks. If Christmas Eve is on a Sunday the first Sunday in Advent will fall on December 3, and the fourth Sunday of Advent coincides with Christmas Eve. Before you make an Advent calendar count the number of days in Advent in that year.

  There are many kinds of Advent calendars. The most common are those in which a child opens one door for each day of Advent. Advent calendars help children anticipate Christmas, enabling them to count the days, even in some versions, making visible the approach of Christmas. Advent is the festival of expectation. The colour blue can be seen to express expectation, so it is a colour appropriate for Advent.

An Advent ladder

❖ *A piece of blue cardstock about*
    25 × 35 cm (10" × 14")
  2 wooden slats about 7 × 7 and 310
    mm long (¼" × ¼" × 12¼")
  Gold cardstock or cardboard
  Gold paper for the stars
  Rose-coloured beeswax
  Half a walnut shell
  A little teased sheep's wool
  Glue

• Round off the top corners of the blue card.

Calendars

- Sandpaper the slats till they are smooth and stick them to the middle of the blue card about 1 cm (³/₈") from the bottom and 6 cm (2³/₈") apart.
- Cut two long struts 1 cm (³/₈") wide and 31 cm (12¼") long, and as many golden rungs 7 × 0.4 cm (2¾" × ³/₁₆") from the gold card as there are days in Advent including the first Sunday of Advent and Christmas Eve.
- Before sticking on the rungs, mark their places on the wooden slats — the distance between each rung should be about 13 mm (½"). Stick the rungs on, starting at the top and working down. Once all the rungs are firmly glued on, stick the gold card struts on to the slats so that they cover the rung-ends. Round off the tops of the struts which project beyond the slats.
- Model the figure of a baby from beeswax so that it can lodge between the rungs. It is advisable to make the child all of one piece rather than making limbs separately and then attaching them.

Figure 83-1.

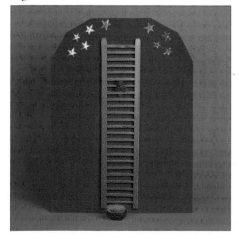

- Place the walnut shell with a little sheep's wool in it at the bottom of the ladder for the crib.
- From the gold paper cut out as many stars as there are days in Advent. Each day the children can stick a star on the blue sky behind the ladder as the Child descends a rung. On Christmas Day the Child lies in the crib while behind him there is a sky full of stars.

Star-ribbon

❖ *130 cm (4 ft) dark blue ribbon 2 cm (¾") wide*
  Silver cardstock or cardboard
  Gold cardstock or cardboard
  Straws
  Fine gold thread
  Glue

Ribbon and a number of stars make a kind of stairway down which an angel can come. Each Advent Sunday is marked by a straw star and the six days between are marked by a silver star; the ladder therefore begins with the first straw star.

- As with the Advent ladder, count the number of days in Advent for the year. Stars should be made for the right number of days.
- The construction of straw stars is fully described on page 92 and a there is a pattern for a five-pointed star on page 115.
- First lay out the straw stars and the silver card stars beside the ribbon to ensure that the distance between the stars is roughly the same.
- Stick all the stars to the ribbon, making sure that you only glue the middle of the star so that the points are not stuck down.
- Finally, cut out an angel from the gold card. Beginning on the first

Sunday of Advent, the angel comes down one step each day, lodging behind the stars neatly, because the points of the stars are not stuck down.
- You can place a crib at the bottom of the ribbon, or you can hang the ribbon above the stable where at Christmas the Child will be born.

Advent walnut chain

❖ *As many walnuts as there are days in Advent*
  Gold paint
  3–4 metres (yards) of red or blue ribbon 2 cm (¾") wide
  Small presents to put in the nutshells
  Glue

- Open the nuts carefully so as not to crack or break the shells. Remove the

Figure 83-2.

kernel. Keep the two halves of each nut together so that they don't get muddled up.

• Paint the outside of the nuts gold and leave them to dry. In one half of each nut place a small present such as a little bell, a dwarf, a shell, a little sheep, a hare of teased sheep's wool, a little stone, a little lump of soft beeswax, a marble, a gold-foil star, a dried flower, a bead, and so on.

• Apply a little glue to each half and stick them together with the ribbon running through the two halves.

• During Advent a nut is cut off the ribbon each day and opened.

A starry sky as Advent calendar

❖ *A big sheet of dark blue construction paper or cardstock*
  Gold paper for the stars
  Glue
  A pair of scissors

• Round off corners of the blue card to indicate the vault of heaven. Place the card in a suitable place, pin it to the wall, or it can form the background to a tableau for a Christmas crib.

• Each day one child, or every child in the family, is allowed to stick a star in the sky. In this way you will have a glorious starry sky as a background to the Christmas crib.

• Older children can cut the stars out themselves.

19 Wreaths

Advent wreath

❖ *Thick wire (2 mm, $^1/_{16}$") for the hoop*
  Thin wire (1 mm, $^1/_{32}$") for the candle-holders
  Sprigs of green fir
  Waxed thread or string
  Four candles
  A blue ribbon

Figure 84-1.

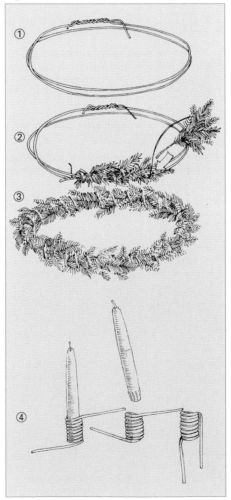

① Take a piece of thick wire the length of which is more than twice the circumference of the Advent wreath, to make a double hoop. Twist the ends firmly together.

② Cover the frame with greenery. Start by making a foundation with larger twigs, 20–25 cm (8"–10"). Lay the bottom of the first stem against the hoop and bind it on with the waxed thread or fine string. Lay the next twig underneath the first so that it is overlapped by the first and bind it on. Continue in this way so that the wreath gradually increases in thickness.

③ After the first round use smaller sprigs which are less stiff and more easily bound on. For the last round use short beautiful sprigs to give a smooth and even effect.

④ For each of the four candle-holders take a piece of thin wire and wind it several times round the bottom of a candle and then bend the two ends down.

• Place the candle-holders on four points of the wreath making sure that they don't disappear into the greenery but remain visible. Bend the protruding ends of wire round the bottom of the wreath.

• Cut the blue ribbon in two equal lengths. Tie the ends of both ribbons on to the wreath midway between the candles.

• Suspend the Advent wreath by the ribbon. If it is not to be hung the blue ribbon can be wound around the wreath as a decoration.

Pine-cone wreath

❖ *7 pine-cones of the same size*
  Thin wire
  A length of ribbon
  A pair of pliers

① Lay the seven well-dried pine-cones out in a circle and measure a length of wire 2½ times the circumference of the circle of cones.
② Bend the wire double.
③ Make an eye at the bend by twisting the wire round several times. The eye is to suspend the wreath. The length of twisted wire between the eye and the first cone should be about 1 cm (½").
④ Push the wire between the scales of the first cone about a quarter of the way up from the bottom, twist the wire a few times so that the pine-cone sits firmly between the wires.
⑤ Attach the other cones in the same way.
● Make sure you twist the wire sufficiently between each cone so that they are not too close together, otherwise you will not be able to bend the wire round to make a wreath.

● Once all seven pine-cones have been attached bend the whole thing round to make a wreath. Twist the end of the wire a few times round the eye and cut off.
● Finish off the wreath by tying a bow with the ribbon under the eye. You could also tie in some greenery.

A simple door wreath

❖ *Waxed thread or a spool with string*
  Green fir sprigs
  Coniferous greenery
  Wire (³/₆₄", 1.5 mm)
  Various kinds of evergreen for decoration such as holly, coniferous greenery, sprigs of spruce fir, ivy, berries, pine and larch-cones, lichen, etc.

● Make a ring of wire about 25 cm (10") in diameter, twisting the ends firmly together (Figure 85-2). First attach some larger fir twigs (20–25 cm, 8"–10" long) as described for the Advent wreath (Figure 84-1).

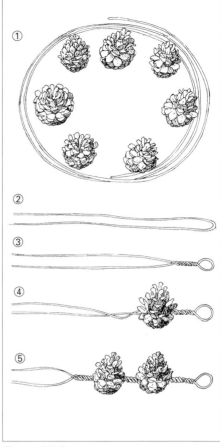

Figure 85-3.

Figure 85-1.

Figure 85-2.

Figure 85-4.

• Use plenty of greenery and pull the wire tight. Avoid protruding twigs. After the foundation of fir twigs continue with coniferous greenery until the wreath has been built up evenly all round.

• Continue building the wreath using the wire for support and covering any visible parts of the wire. Use smaller sprigs of greenery and arrange them evenly with an overlap. Give attention to the blend of colours.

• Attach pine-cones, larch-cones, berries and lichen, by winding a 15 cm (6") piece of wire under the lowest row of scales on the cone. Pull the wire tight and twist it round a few times with a pair of pliers. Lichen can be attached similarly.

• Finally tie a coloured ribbon to the wreath by which it can be suspended.

20 Lanterns

A simple lantern

❖ *1 sheet of thin drawing-paper*
  (120 gsm)
  Water-colours and brush
  Salad oil
  Glue
  A wide jam pot
  A candle

The lantern consists of a loose cuff of paper placed over the jam pot (Figure 86-1 ①).

• Wet the paper, lay it on a board and smooth it out by wiping a wet sponge over it.

• Paint the wet paper with water-colours. Don't paint a picture, just create a mood with the colours.

• Allow the paper to dry and oil both sides of the paper sparingly with cooking oil.

• Cut the paper to the right size. The depth of the paper should be slightly more (but not more than 1 cm, ½") than the height of the glass. The length of the paper should be about 2 cm (¾") more than the circumference of the glass.

① Glue the ends of the paper together to make a cylinder which will fit easily over the glass jar.

• Place a night-light or a small candle in the jar and the lantern is finished.

Variation

② Instead of the jar use a round Camembert cheese-box. Cut away half of the (usually high) rim and remove the top of the lid.

• Glue the upper and lower rims and stick the painted paper first to the bottom half and then on to the top half of the cheese-box. Finally glue the vertical edges of the paper together.

• Take a strip of aluminium foil, fold it several times, and wrap it round a small candle, so that it extends below the candle. Make several cuts in the foil so that it can be spread open in rays and glue them to the bottom of the lantern.

Figure 86-1.

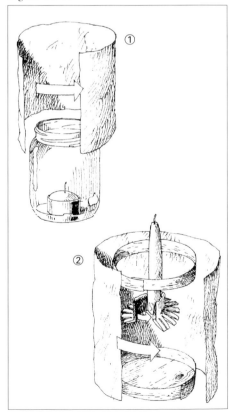

Glass jar lantern

❖ *A large glass jar (2 litre, 2 quarts)*
Tissue-paper in various colours
A piece of gold cardstock or cardboard
An old cloth
Wallpaper glue
A sharp knife or a needle

● Glue a layer of white tissue-paper as a base for the transparency around the outside of the jar. It does not need to be smooth all over.

● Copy the picture in Figure 87-1 or sketch your own design on a piece of paper. Don't make the figures too small.

● Tear or cut the garments out of tissue-paper. Stick the figures flat on the white tissue-paper. Put a fold or two in the clothes. Kings can have golden crowns on their heads and even golden staves in their hands.

● Use blue tissue-paper for the sky. To make a starry sky scratch out stars here and there in the tissue-paper with a sharp knife or a big needle.

● A large jar needs a bigger candle. A night-light is too dim.

A star lantern

❖ *Thin but strong drawing-paper*
(170 gsm)
A pair of compasses or a protractor
A ruler
A knife
A night-light
A glue-stick

This lantern requires eleven pentagons. Use the pattern in Figure 114-1.

● Paint the paper with water-colours before drawing the pentagons and cutting them out.

① Bisect all the sides of the pentagons. Join these points together, scratching along the lines carefully with a knife.

② Fold over the triangles thus obtained to make a smaller pentagon.

③ Stick the pentagons together in such a way that the flaps — the folded corners — always overlap the adjoining pentagon.

④ First construct the bottom half from the base and then build up the upper edge by sticking the pentagons

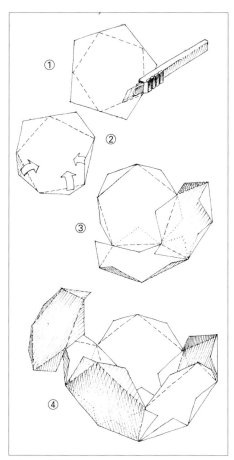

Figure 87-3.

point downward on to the bottom half. On the top edge the flaps are stuck inside; do the same at the bottom if you don't wish to have a base; without a base the candle or night-light is more easily lit.

● When the candle is lit inside the five-star lantern a five-pointed star becomes visible in every pentagon (Figure 87-2).

Figure 87-1.

Figure 87-2.

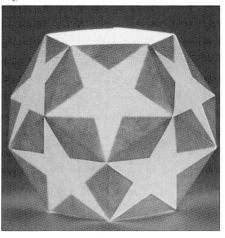

A lantern in the form of a dodecahedron

❖ *Strong drawing-paper (160 gsm)*
  A pair of compasses or protractor
  A ruler
  A knife
  A glue-stick

This lantern looks like the star lantern, but without the five-pointed stars.
• Make smaller pentagons with sides of 5 cm (2"). The pattern in Figure 115-3 gives you an exact pentagram. Figure 109-3 shows (at 60% of true size) how to cut several pentagons from one sheet, to save sticking them together.
① Cut out two lots of five pentagrams (ignore the odd sixth one in Figure 109-3). Fold the flaps inwards and glue them to each other. In this way they are invisible when the light shines through.

② Stick the pentagons of the top and bottom halves together by folding their flaps inward in the same way.

• This lantern too can be painted before drawing and cutting out the pentagons or can be covered with tissue-paper (Figure 88-1).

Figure 88-2.

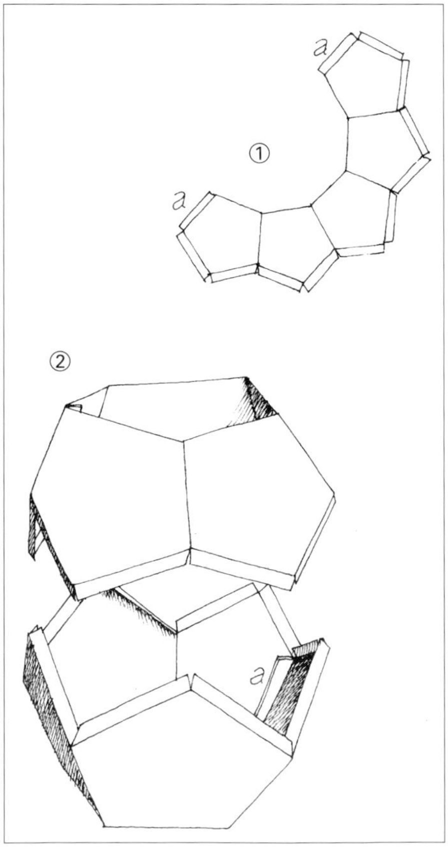

Figure 88-1.

21 Angels

Woollen angel

❖ *Teased sheep's wool, about 45 cm (18") in length*
  Thin gold or silver thread

① When working with teased sheep's wool don't cut it, but pull it apart (Figure 89-1).
② Separate off one third of the wool for the arms and wings of the angel.
③ Tie a knot in the middle of the thicker skein and pull it tight. This becomes the face.
④ Hold the skein vertically letting the wool above the knot fall down.
⑤ Spread this wool round the head as hair and secure at the neck with a long gold thread. Tie the ends of the gold thread together to make a loop for suspending the figure.
⑥ Lay the angel face down. Take the wool which you have just brought down for hair and divide it into three parts. Bring the middle part back up

Figure 88-3.

over the head, bring the other two parts to the sides — they will shortly become the wings.

⑦ For one of the arms separate off a bit of wool about 15 cm (6") long from the thin skein. Twist the wool firmly together in the middle, fold the skein double and tie up the hand with gold thread. Do not cut off the fluff forming the arms. Make the other arm in the same way.

⑧ Keeping the angel face down, place the arms under the neck and bring the tuft of wool which you laid over the head down over the arms.

⑨ Turn the angel over, push the arms and wings well up, and tie up the body firmly under the arms with a length of gold thread. Allow the ends to hang down as tassels from the belt.

⑩ Fluff the wings and robe into shape by holding the wool firmly in one hand and teasing it out carefully with the other.

Angel-mobile

❖ *White tissue-paper*
  Teased sheep's wool
  Gold thread
  White yarn
  Silvered filigree wire or fine wire
  A walnut shell
  White beeswax
  Glue
  A pair of scissors
  A pair of pliers

• Cut out two square pieces 18 × 18 cm (7" × 7") from the tissue-paper. Lay one of the two squares shiny side down on the table with one of the

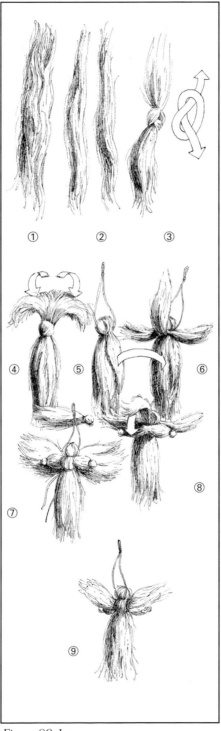

Figure 89-1.

corners pointing away from you (Figure 89-2).

① Fold the left and right corners 2.5 cm (1") inwards.

② Put a blob of wool the size of a big marble in the middle of the square.

③ Fold the paper over the blob so that the two opposite corners meet.

④ Shape the blob and tie off the head with a white thread.

⑤ Make hands out of the two corners of the paper and tie them up with a white thread. Give the angel shape, making the upper part billow out so that she really appears to sweep through the air.

• Take two 20 cm (8") lengths of gold thread and tie one to each hand. Tie the other ends of the two threads together and glue them to the rim of the walnut shell. Take care that the threads are of equal length.

Figure 89-2.

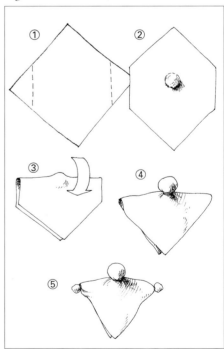

- Make a second angel in the same way and glue the threads to the other side of the walnut.
- Cut a length of 17 cm (7") from the filigree wire and with the pliers bend back both ends of the wire to make loops. Bend the wire to make a slight bow. Tie a gold thread about 17 cm (7") long round the neck of both angels, this is important for the equilibrium of the mobile. Tie these threads to the loops of the wire. Tie a gold thread to the middle of the wire to suspend the mobile.
- Stuff a tuft of wool into the walnut shell (which can be painted gold) and lay a little beeswax child in it. Now the angels can bear the child down from heaven to the earth.
- You could make the angels independently, or alternatively make a mobile with more angels.

Figure 90-1.

A straw angel

❖ *Straws*
  Strong thread or gold thread
  Adhesive tape
  A piece of gold foil
  Glue
  A pair of scissors

- See page 92 for various ways of preparing the straws.
- For the *head* and body use *unironed round straws.*
- For the *arms* use *ironed but not cut open straws.*
- For the *wings* use straws which are *cut open and ironed flat.*
- For the head take about eight unironed round straws and allow them to soak in a basin of water for some hours to make them more pliant.

① Bend the straws over in the middle. The length of the halved straws now makes up the head, body and lower half of the angel.
② Tie off the head with a strong thread.
③ Take three or four ironed (not cut open) straws and insert them between the round straws of the body to form the arms.
④ Tie off the body.

⑤ Now form the straws which make up the lower part of the angel into a round bell-shape using something round, for example a little medicine bottle or a candle (diameter 1.5–2 cm, ¾"), inserting it into the bottom of the bell of straws, so that the wet straws are made to stand out. Stick the straws on to the medicine bottle with adhesive tape that can be removed easily afterwards.
- Allow the straws to dry overnight in this position and next day remove the tape. The straws will now form a round bell.
⑥ Trim the bottom with scissors, but don't cut too much off. Test whether the angel will stand properly by placing her on the table.
- Finish off the arms by gluing the arm straws together and bending them forward before the glue dries.

- At this point these straws have not yet been trimmed and the angel has very long arms. In fact you can now tie these arms together with a bit of string to hold them in front. Once the glue is completely dry trim the arms to the proper length and make hands by tying the ends of the straws together with a thread.

⑦ While the angel's body is drying you can make the wings. Take flat, opened straws, selecting some whole straws of the same colour.

- Lay them across each other in a fan-shape and glue. Dry them under pressure, so that the fan is as flat as possible. You can use adhesive tape here to keep the wings in shape.
- Before attaching the wings dress the angel with a girdle made of a strip of gold foil (as in Figure 91-2), with two golden bands crossing over the breast, or with a golden headband which can have a star.

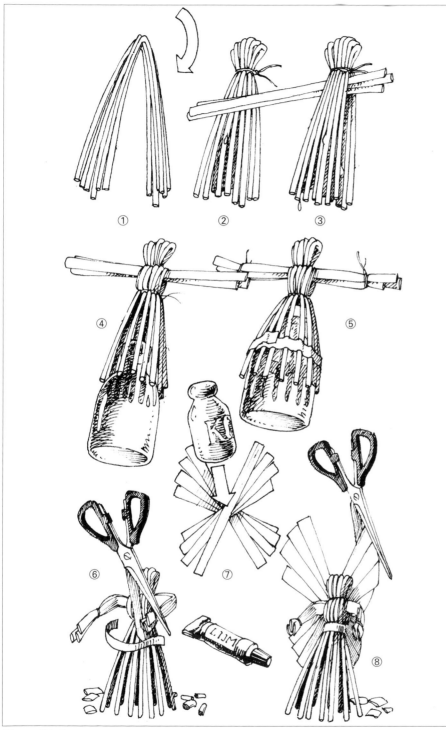

Figure 91-1.

⑧ Glue the fan on to the back of the angel's body to form the wings. When the glue is dry clip the wings to the correct shape.

● The number of straws determines the thickness of the angel. Don't use less than eight straws for the body or the lower part will be too thin.

Figure 91-2.

An angel made of gold foil

❖ *White tissue-paper*
Teased sheep's wool
Gold foil
A blunt needle or fine knitting-needle
Glue

① Cut a square piece of tissue-paper
10 × 10 cm (4" × 4") for the head
② Using a little ball of teased sheep's
wool make the square into a little
head as described for the angel-mobile
(page 89).
③ Tie the head at the neck with
thread.
● Cut out the pieces for the body,
arms and wings (see pattern, Figure
114-2).
④ Lay the gold foil with the outside
uppermost on a base that is not too
hard, for example on a piece of soft
cardboard, and drawing the forms on
the foil with a large blunt needle or a
fine knitting-needle.

⑤ Attach the head by placing the
neck inside the body and sticking the
two edges of the body together to
make a kind of funnel.
⑥ Stick the arms to both sides of the
body, and the wings to the back. Take
a little tuft of teased sheep's wool,
spread this round the head for hair
and glue it on. Finally make two little
hands of tissue-paper and stick these
to the arms.

Figure 92-3.

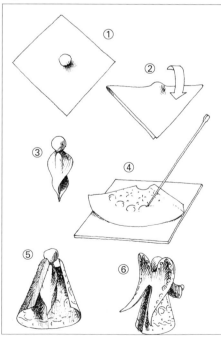

Figure 92-1.

22 Straw Stars

❖ *Straws of natural colour*
A sharp knife
Pointed scissors
A basin of water
An iron

Preparation

● Soak the straws in water for about
an hour. Cut down into the tops a little way with a sharp knife and iron
them open further with a hot iron.
You can also leave the wet straws
uncut and iron them flat straight
away.
● Both the cut-open and the ironed
straws can be made into very wide or
into very narrow strips (cut with a
ruler and a sharp knife). Straw stars
made of cut-open straws have the disadvantage that they have a good side
and a less good side, so that they look
best against a background.
● Straw stars made from straws which
have not been cut open are the same
on both sides, and so are more suitable for mobiles, for use on the
Christmas tree or to be hung in front
of a window.
● In the examples given in this book
gold thread is always used for suspending the stars; but any other
colour can be used, for instance, red.
● Cut the straws into two or three
lengths depending on the size of the
star.

Figure 93-1.

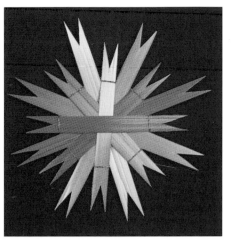

Figure 93-2.

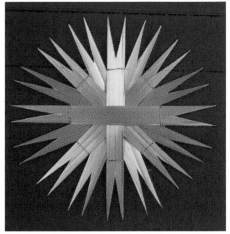

Figure 93-3.

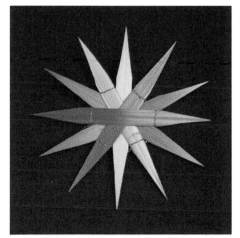

Figure 93-4.

Figure 93-5.

Figure 93-6.

∨ *Figure 93-7.*

∨ *Figure 93-8.*

∨ *Figure 93-9.*

Figure 96-1.

Figure 96-2.

straw make a cross enclosing the other straws.

- The thread with which the star is woven together comes from behind and goes over the last laid straw, under the next straw and so on (Figure 93-4).

Stars with twenty-four and thirty-two points

- For the star with twenty-four points lay one twelve-pointed star on another (Figure 94-3), weave a thread through them and tie them together. Cut off the surplus thread.

    Figure 93-7 shows a large and a small star combined to make a star with twenty-four points.

Variation with 24 points
The star in Figure 93-9 uses three wide and nine long narrow straws
① First lay the three wide straws on top of each other.
② Lay the three narrow straws behind them.
③ Lay two straws against the star in front in the gaps between the narrow and the wide straws.
- Finally bind them together.

Variation with 32 points
This star is made in the same way as the one with twenty-four points, except that two stars with sixteen points are used. A similar star can also be made from four eight-pointed stars. (Figures 93-8, 96-1, 2 and 3)

< *Figure 96-3.*

Great star with sixty-four points

This straw star (Figure 95-2) is made with 32 whole (unironed) straws. In this case the straws are worked while still *wet,* as they are more pliable and break less easily.
- Make a star of eight straws by laying them crosswise on top of each other and tying them up. Make a second star in the same way.
- Lay one star on top of the other, so that the rays interlock. Tie the star together with a fresh thread. The result is a star with thirty-two points.
- Make a second star with thirty-two points, lay one star on top of the other and tie them together with a fresh thread, to make the star with sixty-four points.
- The straws must still be wet when you finish the ends.

Figure 96-4.

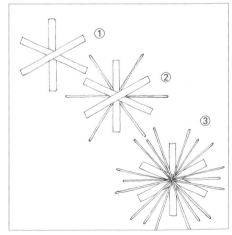

Straw star mobile

This mobile (Figure 95-3) has a large star of David with twelve twelve-pointed stars.

This mobile can be hung during the time between Christmas and Three Kings' Day (January 6). Begin with the large star of David and each day add a twelve-pointed star.

• For the star of David take six wet whole straws.
① Lay three straws on top of each other to make an equilateral triangle and tie the ends together. With the other three straws make a similar triangle.
② Lay one triangle on top of the other to make the six-pointed star of David. Tie the stars together where they cross and suspend the mobile from four points.

• Make the twelve-pointed stars from whole straws ironed flat: since these are heavier they hang well.

Figure 97-1.

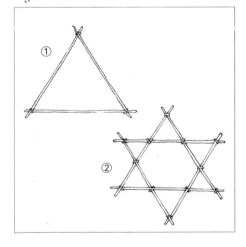

23 Folded Transparent Stars

General instructions

❖ *Kite-paper (transparency paper) or tissue-paper*
Transparent glue or a glue-stick
Double-sided adhesive tape
A sharp knife

Transparent stars are made by folding each piece of transparent paper into a single star-point and then assembling these single star-points to make a star.

Kite-paper (transparency paper) is sufficiently transparent and is more robust than tissue-paper, so it is more easily worked.
Tissue-paper is less colour-fast than kite-paper and since transparent stars are usually left to hang for a long time, tissue-paper stars can quickly lose their colour in the increasing strength of the sunlight.

When choosing the colours remember that the pattern in the transparent stars emerges from the different layers of paper laid upon each other. For complicated stars dark colours are not suitable, use yellow, orange, pale green or rose.

Do not make the stars too small because it is more difficult to make the folds exact. The examples in this book have a diameter of 20 cm (8").

The proportion of the sheets is important — if it is altered, the pattern changes too. For example Figures 101-1 uses 10 × 7.5 cm (4" × 3") sheets while Figure 101-2 uses 10 × 4.5 cm (4" × 1¾") sheets.

• Before making the star-points experiment with:
• *Oblong sheets* (for instance 10 × 7.5 cm, 4" × 3"). Here the length of the sheet determines the dimensions of the star. In our examples (page 101) the star will be twice the length, that is 20 cm (8").
• *Square sheets* where the diagonal determines the dimensions of the star. A sheet 7.5 × 7.5 cm (3" × 3") has a diagonal of a little over 10 cm (4") — about one third longer than the sides.

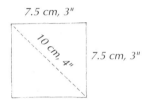

7.5 cm, 3"

10 cm, 4"

7.5 cm, 3"

7.5 cm, 3"

• Work out beforehand how many pieces can be obtained from one large sheet to avoids waste. You can get a 100 hundred oblong sheets (10 × 7.5 cm, 4" × 3") or 130 square sheets (7.5 × 7.5 cm, 3" × 3") out of a 75 × 102 cm (30" × 40") sheet of kite-paper.
• Make sure that the pieces are exactly the same size; to achieve this, first fold the large sheet exactly in two (with a sharp crease) and slit in two with a sharp knife. Then fold these two sheets in two and cut them. Continue in this way until you have obtained the desired size. A guillotine or trimmer is very useful for this. In order to obtain a different shape of sheet, narrower, wider or longer, first cut a strip off the large sheet, so that exact measurements are obtained.

- It is important to fold the sheets as exactly as possible because any divergence shows up in the final result.
- The creases must be really sharp. When the same points have to be folded twice as in Figure 101-3 ② then don't make the first fold come exactly to the centre line but leave a tiny gap. Ensure that the sides come exactly together with the second fold.
- Stick down all the folded parts using transparent glue, adhesive or a glue-stick. Non-transparent adhesive becomes visible when the star is hung up. Make sure that you don't use too much glue on the paper.
- Finally stick the stars to the window with strips of double-sided adhesive tape. Use only very small strips and stick them to the parts where the star is least transparent (the points) then the tape will not be seen. If the strips of adhesive tape are too large it is difficult remove the star without damaging it.

Stars from square pieces

With stars made from square pieces the diagonal is the central fold.

Simple eight-pointed star

❖ *8 square pieces of kite-paper*
   (7.5 × 7.5 cm, 3" × 3")

① Fold the sheets across the diagonal so that points B and C meet. Unfold again.
② Fold points B and C in to the diagonal; stick them down with a spot of glue.
③ When all eight sheets are folded in this way stick the star carefully together, with the unfolded base of the first star-point to the diagonal of the next continuing until all the points have been stuck together (Figure 99-3).

Ten-pointed star

❖ *10 square pieces of kite-paper*
   (7.5 × 7.5 cm, 3" × 3")

- Fold the star-points in the same way as before (Figure 98-2 ① and ②).
- Stick the unfolded base of the second star-point a little bit over the diagonal of the first as in Figure 99-1 ②. This forms a pattern of rays in the heart of the star (Figure 99-4).

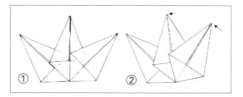

Figure 98-1.

Eight-pointed star

❖ *8 square pieces of kite-paper*
   (7.5 × 7.5 cm, 3" × 3")

This eight-pointed star is a slight variation (Figure 99-1).
① Crease the diagonal, fold points B and C to the diagonal.
② Unfold again.
③ Fold points B and C to the newly made crease, close the flaps again, and stick down securely.
- Then stick the star together as in Figure 98-2 ③ to result in Figure 99-5.

Figure 98-2.

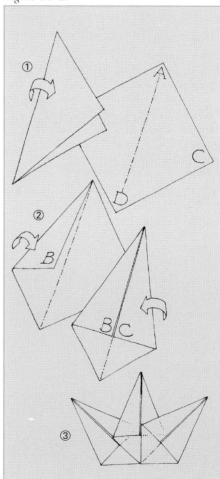

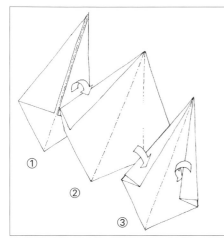

Figure 99-1.

Figure 99-3.

Figure 99-4.

A five-pointed star

❖ *5 square pieces of kite-paper (7.5 × 7.5 cm, 3" × 3")*

By taking *five* instead of *eight* star-points you can modify the star in Figure 99-5 to make Figures 99-6 and 99-7.

● The overlap of each individual point of the star is no longer a half point as before, but only a tiny bit (about 10–12 mm, ½"). In this way a five-pointed motif appears in the middle (Figure 99-6).

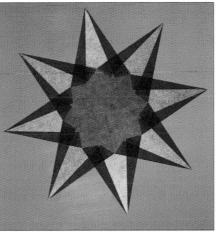

Figure 99-5.

Figure 99-6.

Figure 99-7.

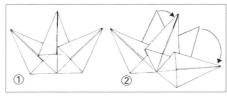

Figure 99-2.

A ten-pointed star

❖ *10 square pieces of kite-paper*
   (7.5 × 7.5 cm, 3" × 3")

• With ten star-points make two five-pointed stars and stick one on top of the other. This gives you the star in Figure 99-7.
• Alternatively first assemble one five-pointed star and then stick the remaining five points one by one between the points of the star.

Eleven-pointed star

❖ *11 square pieces of kite-paper*
   (7.5 × 7.5 cm, 3" × 3")

• Fold the sheets as in 99-1 ① ②
① Then fold the lower half (that is, the part which will be the centre of the star) towards the diagonal line (Figure 100-2).
② Stick the folds down.
• Stick the eleven star-points these together to produce the star of Figure 100-1. You can see the amount of overlap.rs from oblong sheetWith stars from oblong sheets the centre line is the central fold.

Figure 100-1.

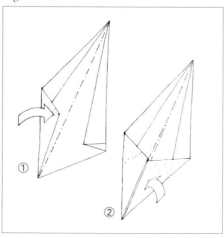

Figure 100-2. >

Figure 101-1.

Figure 101-2.

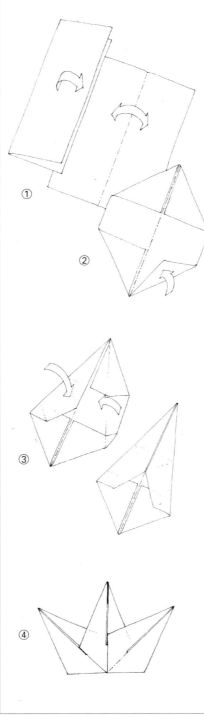

① ② ③ ④

Figure 101-3.

Stars from oblong pieces

With recatngular sheets, it is the length of the sheet which determines the dimensions of the star. Thus the diameter of the star will be 20 cm (8") using sheets of 10 × 7.5 cm, (4" × 3").

Simple eight-pointed star

❖ *8 oblong pieces of kite-paper (10 × 7.5 cm, 4" × 3")*

① Fold the sheets lengthwise and unfold them again.
② Fold the four corners in to the centre line so that a point is made above and below. Stick down the corners with a bit of glue.
③ From the top point fold the two sides once again to the centre line. This sharp point makes one of the points of the star, while the wider lower point will be in the centre of the star.
④ When all eight sheets are folded in this way stick the star carefully together, with the unfolded base of the first star-point to the diagonal of the next continuing until all the points have been stuck together (Figure 101-1).

Eight-pointed star 2

❖ *8 oblong pieces of kite-paper (10 × 4.5 cm, 4" × 1¾")*

• Fold in the same way as above, but with the narrower sheet, you will get the star in Figure 101-2.

Figure 102-1.

Figure 102-2.

Figure 102-3.

Eight-pointed star 3

❖ *8 oblong pieces of kite-paper*
(10 × 7.5 cm, 4" × 3")

① Fold the sheets lengthwise and un-fold them again.
② Fold in only the two top corners to the centre line. Unfold them again.
③ Halve the corner folds and tuck the edge inside as you fold it again.
④ Assemble the star by first using four star-points to make a four-pointed star. Then insert the remaining points be-tween the first four (Figure 102-1).

Figure 102-4.

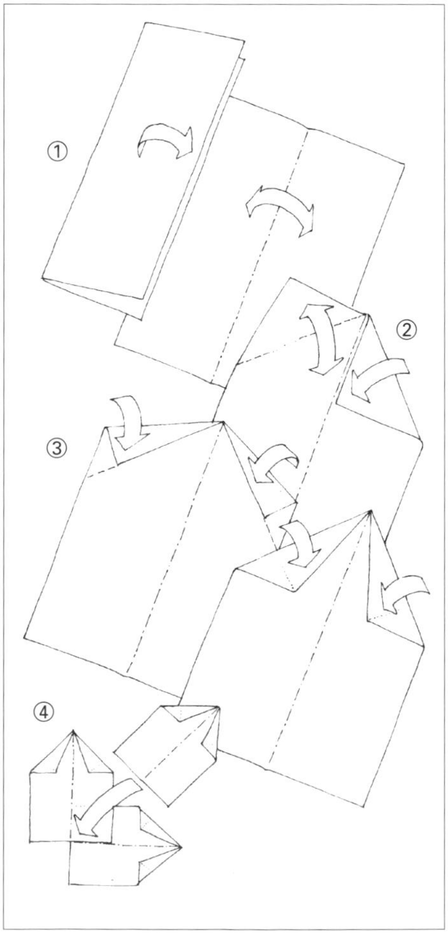

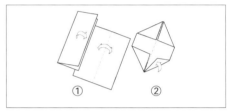

Eight-pointed star 4

❖ *8 oblong pieces of kite-paper*
(10 × 7.5 cm, 4" × 3")

Fold each corner towards the centre line (Figure 102-5).
① Unfold the lower corners again (Figure 103-1).
② Fold the lower two points to the new crease and then fold inwards.
③ Fold the top flap onto the centre crease.
④ Finish by folding the other flap.
● Stick together to make the star in Figure 102-2.

Figure 102-5.

Eight-pointed star 5

❖ *8 oblong pieces of kite-paper*
(10 × 7.5 cm, 4" × 3")

● Fold each corner towards the centre line (Figure 102-5).
① Unfold the lower corners again (Figure 103-2). Find the midpoint of the fold-line by folding carefully diag-onally.
② Then fold the outer point to the midpoint of the fold-line and refold both sides along the fold-line to the middle.
③ Fold the top flap onto the centre crease.
④ Finish by folding the other flap.
● Stick together to make the star in Figure 102-3.

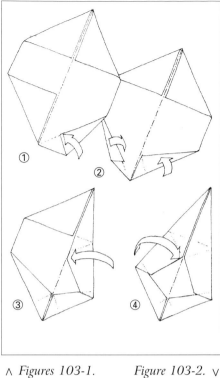

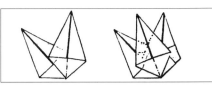

Figure 103-3.

A sixteen-pointed star

❖ *16 oblong pieces of kite-paper (10 × 7.5 cm, 4" × 3")*

• Choose a light colour as there are many layers of paper on top of each other in this star.

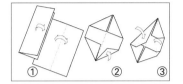

• Fold the pieces as for the *Eight-pointed star 4* (steps ① to ③).
• Stick the star-points as if making an eight-pointed star (Figure 103-3). Then stick one star-point exactly between each of the eight. The result can be seen in Figure 103-4.

∧ *Figures 103-1.*   *Figure 103-2.* ∨

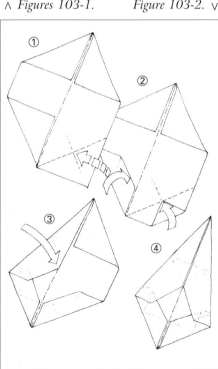

Figure 103-4

Figure 104-1.

Figure 104-2.   Figure 104-3.

Narrow eight-pointed star

❖ *8 oblong pieces of kite-paper
  (12 × 4.5 cm, 4¾" × 1¾")*

The character of the star is quite different because the sheets are narrower.
• Don't use sheets smaller than the above measurements, as they will be too difficult to work,

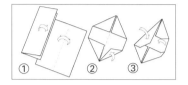

• After the basic folds above, follow Figure 104-4.
① Fold the outside folds again.
② Then fold them again to make a sharp point.
• Stick together to make the star in Figure 104-1.

Narrow sixteen-pointed star 1

❖ *16 oblong pieces of kite-paper
  (15 × 4.5 cm, 6" × 1¾")*

• Fold the star-points in the same way as the above *Narrow eight-pointed star.*
• Stick the star together as described for the previous sixteen-pointed star (Figures 103-3 and 4).
• The final result can be seen in Figure 104-2.

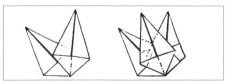

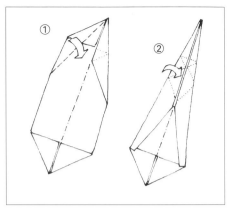

Figure 104-4.

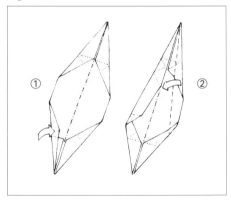

Figure 104-5.

Narrow sixteen-pointed star 2

❖ *16 oblong pieces of kite-paper
  (15 × 4.5 cm, 6" × 1¾")*

In this star an extra fold is added and so a larger size of paper is used (Figure 104-5).
① Fold each of the corners twice.
② Then fold the two outside corners in again to make a sharp point.
• Stick together like the previous one to make the star in Figure 104-3.

24 Nativity Scenes

A clay stable

A clay stable can be made as simply as you wish (Figure 105-2). Children can make this stable by themselves.

- With these simple stables the surrounding "landscape" creates an atmosphere. Use dark brown or green cloth and lay some stones, moss or pine-cones on it. Make trees by sticking a sprig of green in a lump of clay.
- One suggestion is to let the children make something for each Sunday during Advent.
- On the first Sunday they can make the stable.
- On the second Sunday they can make some bushes and trees to go round it.
- On the third Sunday some sheep.
- And on the fourth Sunday the people, Joseph, Mary and the shepherds, and for Christmas the angel and the Child.
- Make the figures in one piece. Do not make arms, legs and head and then stick them on to the body because once the clay dries the separate parts are liable to fall off.
- Once the stable is dry it can be coloured with water-colours if desired.

Stable with shepherds

❖ *White and brown unspun sheep's wool
Pink knitted cotton
Coloured scraps of cloth and felt
Scraps of fur
Unspun wool or camel-hair*

Mary, Joseph, the shepherds and the Child

① For each figure work a tuft of teased white wool into a firm roll approximately 9 cm (3½") long (Figure 105-1).
② Form a round head at one end.
③ Wrap a piece of knitted cotton round it and tie it off to make the head.
④ Make a fairly close-fitting garment from a thicker woollen material or felt to cover the rest of the roll of wool, so that the figure can stand.
⑤ Gather the cloth in at the neck.

- *Mary* has a robe of red felt, with a cloak made of a square piece of blue cloth or felt.
⑥ Drape the cloak round her head and fasten with a few stitches at the head and the neck.
- The hands are made of some teased sheep's wool covered with knitted cotton.
⑦ Sew them on between the folds of the cloak.
- Draw in the eyes and mouth with a fine pencil.

- *Joseph and the shepherds* have capes of cloth or fur. Secure these at the neck and at the centre front with a few stitches. A stick can then be inserted between the cape and the body.
- The hair is made of teased brown sheep's wool secured with the hat.

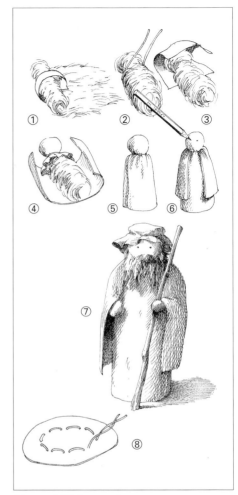

Figure 105-1.

∨ *Figure 105-2.*

⑧ *The hat* consists of a round piece of felt. You can form the hat by gathering it. Sew the hat on to the head with a few stitches.

● *The Child* is made in the same way as the other dolls, only a little smaller. When the head is finished wrap the rest of the body in a cloth of light-coloured material, flannel or felt. Secure the cloth with a few stitches.

● Make the *sheep* from a rectangular piece of fur or fleece. Roll this in from the narrow end. Sew up at the bottom and if necessary at the ends using a leatherwork needle. Tie off about one third to make the head. Now clip the sheep to give it a good shape. Make ears of soft leather or felt and sew them on.

● *Ox and ass* (Figure 106-1). Turn in the ends of a little skein of carded unspun wool; from this form a lying ass with a few loose stitches and a fine thread. Make the ears by gently pulling out the wool.
● For the ox, camel-hair or light brown, teased sheep's wool is very suitable.

● *The stable* can be built of pieces of bark and twigs nailed or stuck together; use single large pieces of bark for the roof. The stable can then be furnished with straw, moss, plants, stones, and so on.

Figure 106-1. Ox and ass.

A sheep

❖ *4 pipe-cleaners*
White unspun wool
A darning-needle
Crochet hook No. 3
An old pair of scissors or pliers
Glue

① For the head of the sheep bend the end of a pipe-cleaner round two fingers and twist it round the neck (Figure 107-1). Make a kink for the neck.
● For the forelegs bend a pipe-cleaner round the body; and do the same for the hindlegs. Cut the feet to shape only when the sheep is completely finished.
② Use the fourth pipe-cleaner to give the frame more stability and to lengthen the tail. Bend the end of the first pipe-cleaner to the front and twist it round the body.
③ Tease a bit of wool out and begin working it round the sheep at the stomach. After each turn let go the tuft to avoid getting it twisted. Continue working round the sheep evenly from the body to the head and back again to the hind parts until it is thick enough.

Figure 106-2. A sheep.

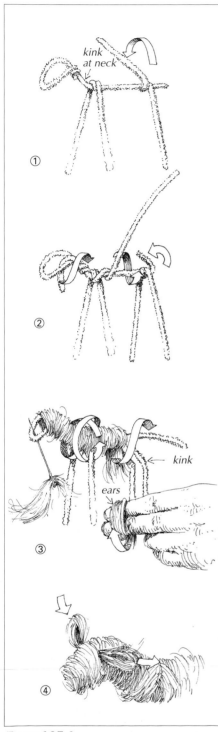

① ② ③ ④

Figure 107-1.

• Keep winding the wool to the last fibre, this will prevent it from unravelling. Do not work to the very end of the nose, or the wool will slip off.

• Work the shoulders and the hindlegs as follows: hold one end of the piece of wool tightly on to the left shoulder, take the wool down behind the left foreleg and back up obliquely over the chest, over the neck, crosswise over the breast to the right foreleg, back behind it and so on. In this way you form a figure of eight. Do not work the wool too tightly and make sure that it lies flat on the back. Work the hindquarters in the same way. Do not make the head too thick.

• *The nose.* Thread a bit of wool through the darning-needle and secure the nose. Cover the front part also with wool.

• *The tail.* Push the wool towards the hindquarters so that the pipe-cleaner of the tail stands free. Wind a tuft of wool over half of the pipe-cleaner.

• Bend the pipe-cleaner back half way, so that the end of the tail is covered with wool. the tail should now be 2.5 cm (1") long. Finish off the bent-back tail with another tuft of wool, giving the tail a nice shape.

• *The legs.* Push the wool of the body up a bit and wind good thin tufts of wool round the legs about halfway down. Put some glue on the lower half of the legs and continue to wind on wool. Allow the glue to dry properly and finish off by cutting the legs to the right size.

④ *The ears.* Wind a bit of wool regularly round two fingers and remove. Thrust the crochet hook carefully through the right place through the head. Catch the wool in the hook and pressing your fingers on the other side of the head pull the hook through.

• Take both ears between your thumb and forefinger and rub them into shape. Let the ears hang and fasten them with needle and thread.

• *Ox and ass* can be made in the same way.

25 Geometrical Figures

❖ *Gold foil*
  A fine pair of scissors or a sharp knife
  A pencil with a sharp point
  Glue
  A ruler

Figure 108-1. (50% of true size).

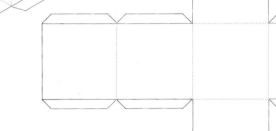

Gold foil tetrahedron

A tetrahedron is a regular solid figure contained by four regular (equilateral) triangles (Figure 108-2). Enlarge the pattern of Figure 108-1 to double its size, or alternatively follow the instructions on page 113 to construct the shapes in any size.

• It is easiest to photocopy the pattern or construct it on a loose sheet of paper. This avoids unnecessary lines and marks appearing on the foil.
• Lay the sheet of paper with the copied pattern on the back of the gold foil, and stick it on with two little bits of adhesive tape so that it will not slip. Then draw in the whole form on to the foil.
• Remove the paper and cut the form out of the foil. To get good sharp creases fold and unfold the crease a few times before sticking down.
• Spread the glue thinly on both surfaces to be stuck. Wait until the glue is nearly dry and then stick the tetrahedron together, sticking a suspension thread to the inside before closing it. Tie a few knots at the bottom of the thread so that it will not slip out of the tetrahedron. Make sure that the corners join together as exactly as possible because the glued parts are not easy to unstick again.

Gold foil cube

A cube consists of six squares. The pattern in Figure 108-3 is half true size. There are instructions for geometrical construction on page 113.
• Stick the cube together in the same way as the tetrahedron.

Figure 108-3. (50% of true size).

Figure 108-2.

Figure 108-4

Gold foil icosahedron

The icosahedron consists of twenty equilateral triangles (Figure 108-4).
• In Figure 109-2 the pattern is shown unfolded at 60% of true size.
• The construction of the icosahedron is as for the tetrahedron.
• Fold all the lines before beginning to glue the model, as this is no longer possible afterwards.
• Leave one of the triangles open to the end, so that you can even out any irregularities from the inside using a pencil.

Gold foil dodecahedron

This figure consists of twelve regular pentagons (Figure 109-1).
• Figure 109-3 shows a pattern (at 60% of true size) for six pentagons which make up half of the dodecahedron.
• When the six pentagons are stuck together they make a bowl. Two such bowls fit exactly together (see Figure 88-2), but in this model only the

lower bowl needs flaps, not both bowls.
• If using this pattern for the lantern (page 88) cut the flaps on *both* parts, also making an extra flap at *a*. When the flaps are glued together they are invisible when the light shines through.
• Stick the bottom-half together completely, and when sticking the top half together, leave the "lid" open.
• If necessary the sticking edges can be pressed with a pencil from the inside and any irregularities removed. Before sticking down the lid stick a thread to the inside of one of the corners.

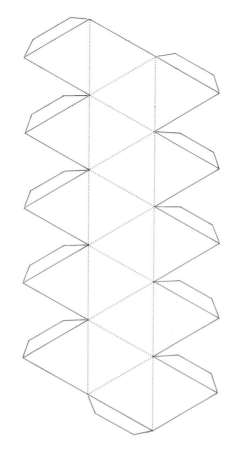

Figure 109-2. (60% of true size).

Figure 109-1.

a

a

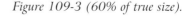

Figure 109-3 (60% of true size).

Three-dimensional gold foil star

From a dodecahedron a three-dimensional star can be made (Figure 110-2).

• Make twelve pentagonal pyramids, the base of each being the same size as that of the dodecahedron (Figure 110-1) and stick one pyramid on to each pentagon.

• In the same way a three-dimensional star can be made from an icosahedron, in this case use twenty three-sided pyramids.

Figure 110-1. (60% of true size).

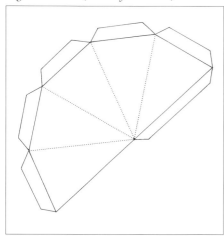

Figure 110-2.

Straw dodecahedron

❖ *Straws*
A ruler
A sharp knife
Elastic adhesive tape
Glue
Some strong paper
A pair of scissors
A little thread

This dodecahedron consists of twelve regular five-pointed stars (Figure 101). As a guide to determining the size of this figure:
the *side* of a pentagon is 1¼" (30 mm)
the *"diagonal"* of a five-pointed star is 5 cm (2")
the *diameter* of the whole dodecahedron will be about 8 cm (3¼").

• Use cut-open ironed straws (see "Straw stars" on page 92). Cut the straws into thin strips with the help of a sharp knife and a (steel) ruler.

• For a dodecahedron sixty (12 × 5) straws are needed. So calculate how many strips can get out of one straw to avoid waste.

• For this three-dimensional form it is

Figure 110-3.

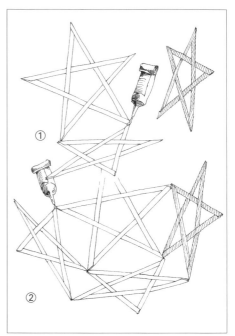

Figure 110-4.

very important that the five-pointed stars are exactly the same size.

Preparation
• A handy way of making the straws all the same size is to mark off the desired length on some drawing-paper.

Figure 110-5.

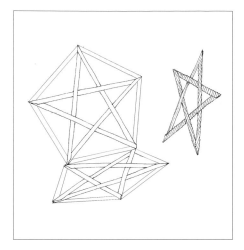

Figure 111-1.

Lay all the straws on the paper between the marks. Stick the straws together with some elastic adhesive tape. Clip them to size with a pair of scissors along the marks.

• Construct a five-pointed star of the desired size on a piece of paper (for the construction see Figure 113-3), or copy it from the Figure 115-3. Use this as a template for sticking the star together.

• Take five straws and lay them with the shiny side down. Select five straws of the same width for each five pointed-star.

• Apply a little glue to the ends of two straws, one on the shiny side, one on the dull side (use a tube with a very fine nozzle, for example model-building glue). Allow the glue to dry a bit and then stick the end of the other straw on to it firmly.

• Figure 110-4 ① shows the five straws interwoven to make a five-pointed star with the third straw worked under one of the two other straws. Apply glue to one of the ends of the two straws stuck together, allow it to dry a bit and stick on the third

straw. In the same way stick the last two straws.

• Quickly check that the star is regular by laying it on the pattern. If necessary adjust the points before the glue sets.

• Make all the stars in this way and allow them to set.

• Now join the stars together to form a dodecahedron by applying a little glue to all five points of the first three stars. Allow the glue to dry a bit.

① Stick two stars together at two points. Place one of these stars on a block of wood as a base and ease the other star up so that the third star can be joined to the pair (Figure 110-4).

• Apply glue to the points of the next three stars and allow to dry.

② Stick these stars to the free points of the three stars already joined. Now half of the dodecahedron is finished.

• Proceed in the same way until the whole star is finished. When you are sticking the last star on use a little more glue on one of the points so that you can attach a gold suspension thread.

Variation 1

• You can join the points of the stars together so that you get a pentagon with a five-pointed star inside it. As these links are always *between* adjoining stars, add them after sticking the stars together.

Variation 2

Figure 110-5 shows a smaller dodecahedron inside a larger one. For this two complete dodecahedrons are needed, the smaller being less than two thirds of the larger.

• Paint the smaller dodecahedron with a little red transparent varnish to make it more visible or to take darker straws for the smaller star.

• Place the smaller dodecahedron inside the larger one before the last two five-pointed stars are stuck together. Stick the thread joining the smaller dodecahedron to the larger ensuring that the distance between them is correct.

A straw ball

❖ *Straws*
   A sharp knife
   Glue
   A gold thread

● Iron the straws flat (see page 92) and cut them into strips about 3 mm (¹/₈") wide. The ball in Figure 112-1 consists of eight rings.

① Because the rings are all stuck over each other the diameter of the innermost ring must be a fraction smaller than that of the next one and so on. As the difference is scarcely perceptible the best way is to stick the two ends of the innermost ring with slightly more overlap than those of the next.

② Make the first two rings, allow them to dry fully and then stick them together in the form of a cross making sure that the joints of the straws don't coincide exactly.

● The glue of these rings stuck together must now dry fully because this is the foundation for the rest.

③ Make the remaining six rings and allow them to dry too. Then fill up

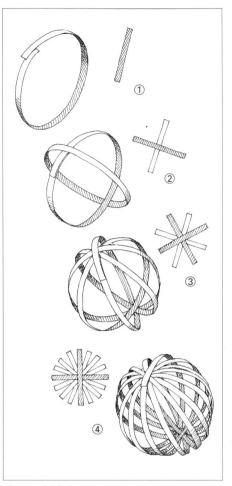

Figure 112-2.

the gaps between the cross in the following way: begin by sticking two rings in the middle between the cross.

④ Once this is quite dry stick the remaining four rings in the intervening spaces.

● Allow the glue to dry properly, then glue a piece of thread on to one of the rings.

● The positioning of the thread produces different images: if it placed as in Figure 112-1 it produces the greatest effect of depth; if attached to the cross-points of the rings there is a vertical effect to the ball, the opposite of the horizontal effect when attached to

the middle of a half. Several identical balls can create the impression that they are all different.

● An extra ring placed at right angles round the other rings can be the beginning of a whole series of variations. The breadth of the rings can also be varied; indeed one can place rings touching each other all the way round so that a true ball is formed.

Figure 112-1.

26 Constructions and Models

The construction of a tetrahedron

① Draw a line and mark on it points A and B. The distance AB determines the size of the tetrahedron. With a pair of compasses draw an arc radius AB, with A as a centre, above and below the line AB. Draw a second arc using B as a centre. The intersection of the arcs gives the points C and D. Join these points to A and B.
② Repeat this construction from A and D, and from B and D; this gives points E and F. Join these new points to the others.
● Finish the tetrahedron by drawing in the tabs for sticking (Figure 108-1).

The construction of a cube

① With a pair of compasses, mark off points A, B, C, D and E at equal intervals along a line. The distance AB determines the size of the cube.
● Draw arcs with radius AC from B and D to make point F and from C and E to make point G.
② From these two points draw vertical lines down to points C and D. Mark the distance CD from C twice on the vertical to find H and K, and similarly find J and L from D.
● Draw a line through H and J, and through points K and L, thus forming three parallel lines.
● Mark distance CD off on the extension of line HJ to make points above A, B and E. Mark the same distance

up the verticals above points H and J.
● Finally draw the tabs for sticking the cube together (Figure 108-3).

The construction of a pentagon

① Draw a circle with compasses.
② Draw a horizontal line through the middle of the circle. Draw a vertical line crossing the horizontal line at the centre of the circle.
③ Find the centre of the line AC by cutting the circle at two points D and E with arcs of the radius of the circle

Figure 113-3.

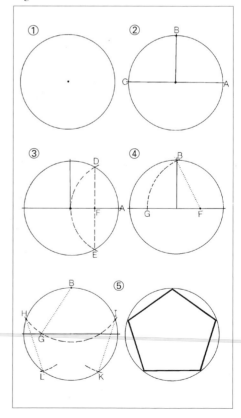

Figure 113-1.

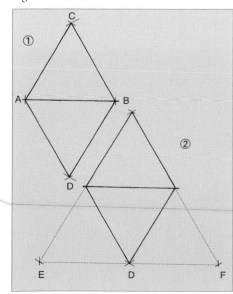

Figure 113-2.

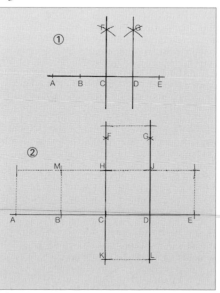

113

and centre *A*. By joining *D* and *E* point *F* is obtained.

④ Mark the distance *FB* on the horizontal centre-line to give point *G*.

⑤ The distance *BG* forms the length of the sides of the pentagon. With centre *B* mark this distance on the circle, to give points *H* and *I*. Mark the same distance off from *H* and *I* on the circle to give points *L* and *K*. The points *B*, *H*, *L*, *K* and *I* form the points of the pentagon.

• This construction is not difficult but as an alternative the pattern opposite has been produced so that you can trace out an exact pentagon from one of the patterns without having to construct it.

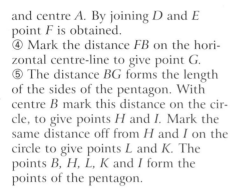

Figure 114-1. Construction of a pentagram.

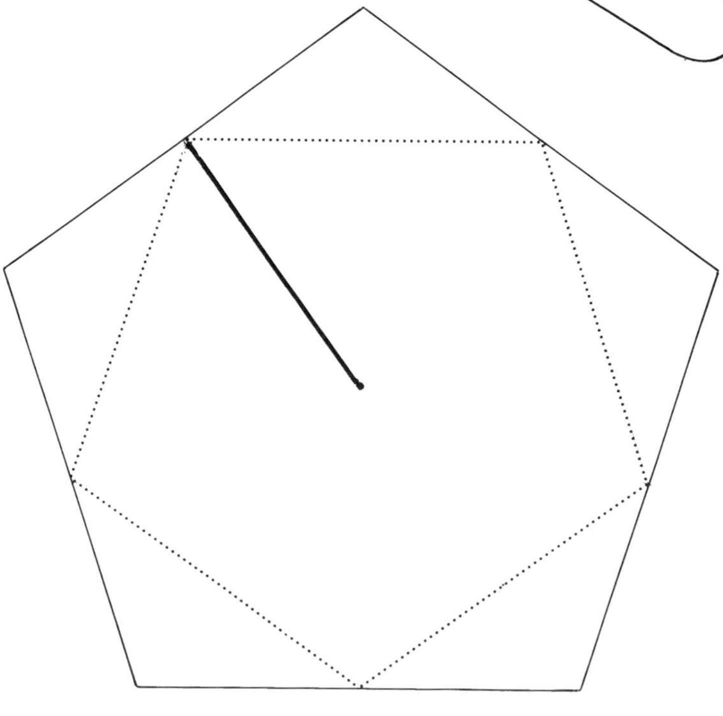

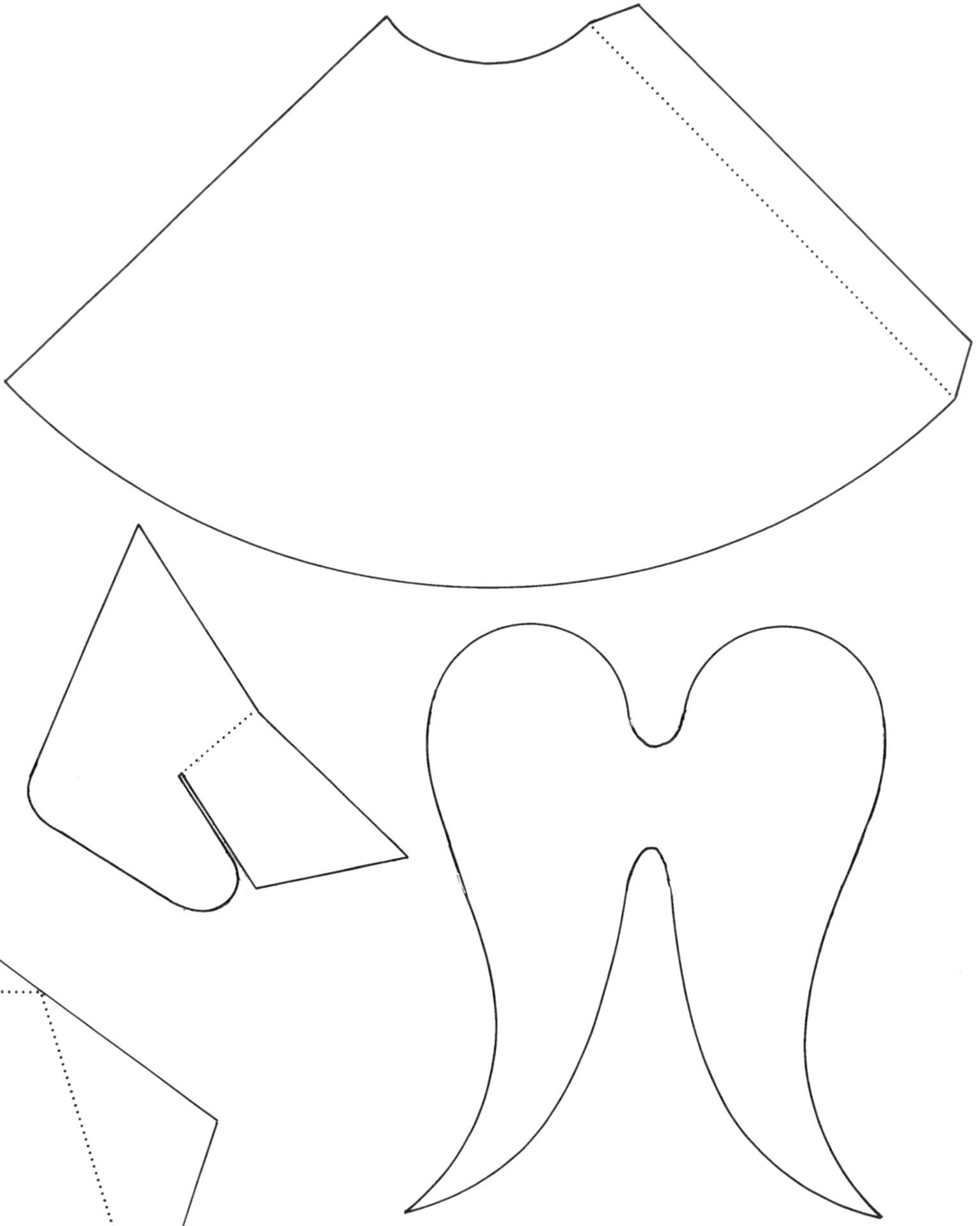

Figure 114-2. Pattern for gold foil angel (page 92).

114

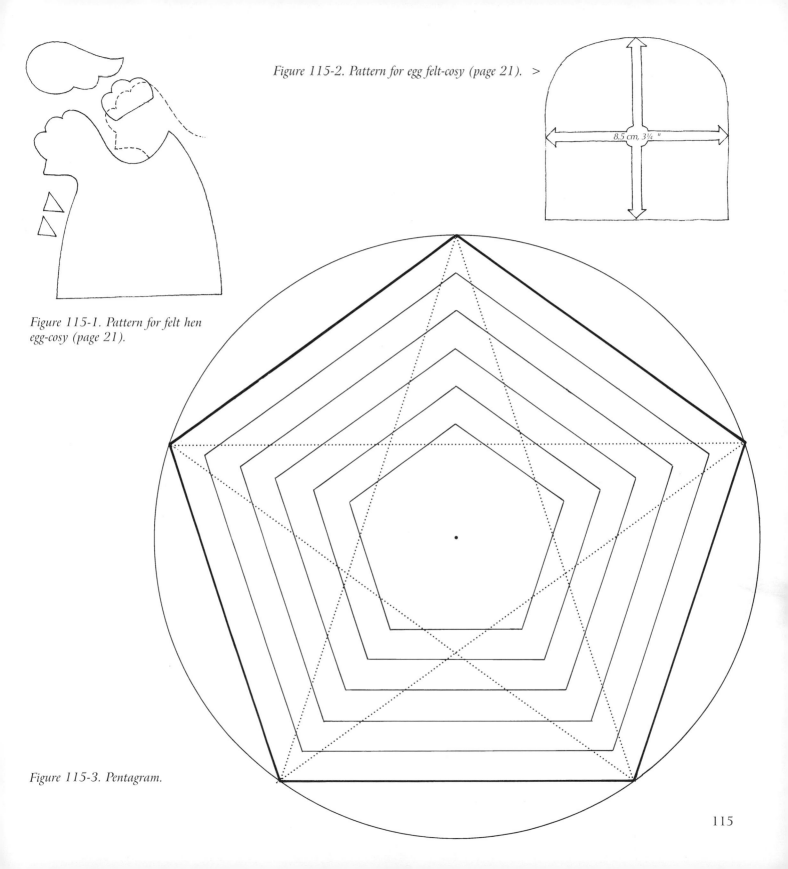

Figure 115-2. Pattern for egg felt-cosy (page 21). >

8.5 cm, 3¼ "

Figure 115-1. Pattern for felt hen
egg-cosy (page 21).

Figure 115-3. Pentagram.

Materials

Basics
A pair of strong scissors for cutting all kinds of things
A pair of small pointed scissors
A pair of small pincers
A pair of small pointed pliers
A gimlet (hand drill)
A sharp knife
A pair of tweezers
A few thick needles

Some of the materials used in this book are not so easy to find, and may take some time to locate.

Dried flowers and leaves
Dried flowers and leaves have to be collected and pressed in the late spring and summer of the previous year. Other material from nature can found in summertime almost anywhere, including in cities. Where the material described does not grow locally, find alternatives.

Stalks for the corn-dollies can be found in the country — ask a farmer.

Make sure all the material is properly dried before storing in a dry place, to avoid mould or rotting.

Greenery for Advent
If you can't find greenery in your own or friends' gardens, look our for clearance work in forestry areas or building sites. Garden centres sometimes sell greenery, though it can be expensive.

Paper and Card
Tissue paper is thin, brightly coloured, semi-transparent paper, available in 15–20 colours.
Kite paper is thicker, shiny coloured, semitransparent paper.
Tracing paper is available in blocks as well as in rolls.
Crêpe paper is stretchable in a variety of bright colours.
For *coloured paper* to decorate eggs with you can use origami paper.
Origami paper is specially cut square paper available in different sizes.
Drawing paper comes in various weights in pads, or larger sizes in loose sheets.
For *thin card* you can use thick cartridge paper.
Board is smooth, about 300 gsm or 3-ply 110 lb cover stock.
Coloured board comes in gold, silver or other colours on one side.

Adhesives
Flour paste can be made up simply by mixing flour with a little water, and is suitable for paper.
Wallpaper glue comes as a powder to be mixed with water. Don't mix too much!
There are various *white water-soluble glues* (polymer medium) available under different names in different countries.
Glue sticks are useful as it is easier to get a thin layer which will not buckle or stain thin paper.
Rubber cement (like Cow gum) is available in tubes or pots. It needs a thin layer pasted on each side of paper or board; leave to dry, and then press the surfaces firmly together. Excess cement can be rubbed away, forming a little spongy ball. The disadvantage is the toxic fumes, and it does yellow with age.
Household cement is a fast drying vinyl-based glue in a tube (like Uhu). It is very strong, but does have drawbacks: flammability, toxic fumes, and it often strings.

Candles and wax
Watch with *candles* not to get the cheapest which are made of loose particles, coated in a layer of wax. When pressed too hard they will crumble, spoiling any decoration.

Beeswax comes in slabs. Break it into smaller bits to melt it quickly.

Modelling wax (for instance Stockmar) is thin slabs of slightly translucent coloured wax.

Decorating wax (for instance Stockmar) is fine wax foils in opaque colours which can be applied to candles to decorate them.

Other materials
Skeins of *teased unspun sheep's wool* can sometimes be bought in craft shops. Alternatively if you need a lot, and are willing to do some hard work, buy a fleece and card it yourself.

Magic wool is carded unspun wool, dyed in different colours.

Straws. Some craft shops may have packets of thick and thin straws for craft work. If they cannot be found there, they must be obtained from a farmer at harvesting time. Cut the straw to avoid nodes in the lengths to be used for making stars. If the straws are to be cut open, thick straws are needed.

Wire
The *copper wire* most commonly used here is 0.8 mm ($^1/_{32}$") in diameter. Thicker wire is used for advent wreaths.

Florist's wire is very thin green or dark brown wire, available in craft shops or garden centres.

Gold thread and *silver filigree wire* come in various thicknesses. They are normally used for making jewellery.

Pipe cleaners are available from tobacconists.